Revolution at a Crossroads

Iran's Domestic Politics
and Regional Ambitions

David Menashri

Policy Paper No. 43

THE WASHINGTON INSTITUTE FOR NEAR EAST POLICY

Published in 1997 in the United States of America by The Washington Institute for Near East Policy, 1828 L Street N.W. Suite 1050, Washington, DC 20036

Library of Congress Cataloging-in-Publication Data

Menashri, David.
    Revolution at a crossroads : Iran's domestic politics and regional ambitions / David Menashri.
    p.   cm. — (Policy papers ; no. 43)
    Includes bibliographical references.
    ISBN 0-944029-68-X
    1. Iran—Politics and government—1979-   I. Title. II. Series:
Policy papers (Washington Institute for Near East Policy) ; no. 43.
DS318.825.M48 1997   97-43152
320.955—DC20   CIP

The Author

David Menashri is a senior research fellow at Tel Aviv University's Moshe Dayan Center for Middle Eastern and African Studies and chair of the university's Department of Middle Eastern and African History. Prof. Menashri, the 1995 Meyerhoff Visiting Fellow at the Washington Institute, was previously a Visiting Fulbright Scholar at Princeton and Cornell Universities. In the late 1970s, he spent two years conducting research and field study in Iran on the eve of the Islamic revolution.

Among Prof. Menashri's previous publications are *Iran: Between Islam and the West* (Tel Aviv: Broadcast University, 1996), *Education and the Making of Modern Iran* (Ithaca: Cornell University Press, 1992), *Iran: A Decade of War and Revolution* (New York: Holmes and Meier, 1990), and *Iran in Revolution* (Tel Aviv: Hakibbutz Hameuhad, 1988). He is also the editor of *The Iranian Revolution and the Muslim World* (Boulder, CO: Westview Press, 1990) and *Central Asia Meets the Middle East* (London: Frank Cass, forthcoming, 1997).

Contents

Acknowledgments

I am deeply indebted to colleagues who have provided significant insights and comments on this paper. Special thanks to Professor Ami Ayalon and Dr. Bruce Maddy-Weitzman, editors of the *Middle East Contemporary Survey*; Dr. David Yerushalmi, Tel Aviv University; Professor Farhad Kazemi, New York University; and Professor Asher Susser and Dr. Martin Kramer, the previous and present directors, respectively, of Tel Aviv University's Moshe Dayan Center. I also wish to thank the Dayan Center's Documentation Center and my research assistant, Ayelet Savyon, who provided all possible assistance.

I likewise express my deepest gratitude to Dr. Robert Satloff, director of The Washington Institute for Near East Policy, who initiated the "Focus on Iran" series, and to the staff of the Institute for making this publication possible. Special thanks go to John Wilner, the Institute's director of publications, who edited it; Daniel Sokol, who served as my research intern in Washington; and Nina Bisgyer, the Institute's office manager.

In addition, the preparation of this paper drew extensively upon research for my chapters on Iran in the *Middle East Contemporary Survey*. I am indebted to the Dayan Center for making available the research materials essential to my ongoing research on Iran. Interested readers will find other aspects of contemporary Iranian affairs developed further in my chapters in the annual survey since 1977.

Finally, this paper uses a simplified system of transliteration that makes allowances for pronunciation. Consequently, some similar Arabic and Farsi words are transliterated differently depending on how they are pronounced. Thus, the Farsi words *velayat* and *mojtahed* are spelled differently from the Arabic words *vilaya* and *mujtahid*. The spellings of commonly-used proper names and Islamic terms, however—such as Saddam Hussein—consciously depart from this system. And, with the exception of the *ayn* and *hamzah*, diacritical marks have been omitted.

David Menashri
Tel Aviv
December 1996

Preface

The Islamic revolution in Iran was undoubtedly one of the most momentous events in recent times—certainly in regional and quite possibly global history. The revolutionary *élan* of activists, their unique method of seizing power, the nature of clerical rule, and their goals and policies since seizing power continue to fascinate observers of contemporary affairs. The importance of Iran, its strategic location, and influence in the Muslim world similarly combined to make the Islamic Republic a special focus of interest for policymakers.

In their first seventeen years in power, the clerics concentrated on two main goals: consolidating their rule and implementing Ayatollah Ruhollah Khomeini's revolutionary ideology, which was supposed to advance the country and improve the situation of the Iranian people—particularly those in the lower strata, who had suffered most under the Shah Mohammad Reza Pahlavi. Though fairly successful in stabilizing its rule, the Islamic regime has thus far proven less effective in implementing its doctrine as a vehicle for resolving the mounting social, economic, and political problems that led to the revolution in the first place. This has been the clerical regime's main challenge in the 1990s.

This Policy Paper, the second in a three-volume series focusing on contemporary Iran, analyzes the evolution of the Islamic regime in Iran since the late 1980s. It delves into the ideological changes, political developments, and economic challenges facing the regime, in an attempt to weigh their influence on Iran's domestic politics and regional ambitions. Many questions regarding the leadership and policies of the Islamic regime remain open. The revolution's future path will surely influence countries with a vested interest in Iran and the entire region, and above all the face of modern Iran. The combined impact of the Islamic revolution and the revolutionary changes in the region and the world (e.g., the Gulf War and demise of the Soviet Union) has not been conducive to clear-cut decisionmaking in Iran. To the contrary, it has manifested itself in Tehran's often ambiguous and contradictory policies. Although definite conclusions are difficult to draw at this stage, it is possible to make some tentative observations about the situation in Iran and its impact on the region.

Other aspects of Iran's domestic and foreign policy—its military build-up and economic decline—are covered in the other two papers in the "Focus on Iran" series; only their impact on wider regime politics (such as the domestic struggle for power, public support for the government, and doctrinal differences among various domestic factions) is discussed here. The limited scope of this survey similarly precluded discussion of other aspects of Iranian politics, such as Iran's external opposition, support for Islamist movements, and relations with neighboring states.

Executive Summary

In their seventeen years in power, the clerics who led the 1979 Iranian revolution have concentrated on consolidating their rule and implementing Ayatollah Khomeini's revolutionary ideology. Thus far, they have proven fairly successful in the former—Khomeini's death in June 1989 was marked by stability and continuity, and presidential and Majlis elections have been held on schedule every four years since. The Islamic regime has proven less effective, however, in applying its revolutionary doctrine to resolve the economic, political, and social problems that fueled popular discontent and led to the revolution in the first place. This remains its main challenge in the 1990s.

Khomeini's doctrine was a departure from Islamic theory and practice of recent centuries and thus, in ideological terms, represented a revolution in modern Islamic thought no less than an Islamic revolution. Moreover, like other revolutionary movements, the clerical regime was forced to adapt to the complex demands of governance. In opposition, Khomeini could theorize about an ideal Islamic state; once in power, he (and even more so his disciples) realized that they had to make compromises as a pragmatic response to the exigencies of the situation. Khomeini himself often sanctioned the primacy of state interests over both revolutionary philosophy and his own Islamic doctrine, and used the coercive power of the state to silence prominent theologians and others who openly opposed the government's policies.

Khomeini's death in 1989 ultimately led to the waning of what was perhaps the Islamic revolution's most profound achievement—the unification of religious and state authority in the person of the Supreme Leader. In a clear deviation from the philosophy of the revolution, the clerical regime gave Iranian national interests primacy over Islamic doctrine, and power gradually moved from theologians to revolutionary "religio-politicians."

THE FACTIONAL POWER STRUGGLE

Once the political clergy were firmly in control, a fierce power struggle emerged among three factions: pragmatists, radicals, and conservatives. The pragmatists, who generally hold executive power and run the state, believe that Iran's primary task is to resurrect its economy in the aftermath of the war with Iraq. They advocate improving ties with the West and "reactionary" Muslim states, and draw their support from Iran's modern middle class, including government employees, technocrats, professionals, and elements of the business community.

By contrast, the radicals are mostly outside of the government and derive their support from younger, more militant clerics and student associations. They advocate strict adherence to revolutionary dogma and view emphasis on the economy as a pretext for pragmatism. The radicals have thus tried to block many of the government's economic and reconstruction initiatives. Their own economic goals stress improving the lives of the dispossessed and promoting Iran's economic independence. The radicals reject the government's bid to improve ties with the West (particularly the United States), and instead advocate increased efforts to expand revolutionary Islam beyond Iran's borders.

Though less vocal than the other two factions, the conservatives are nonetheless influential, deriving their strength from the conservative clergy, *bazaar* circles, and the traditional middle class. Conservatives side with the pragmatists on some issues (such as the economy) but with the radicals on others (such as culture). Thus, they advocate both the strict application of Islamic legal, social, and cultural norms, and the sanctity of private property, freedom for private enterprise, and increased economic interaction with the outside world.

Overall, however, the seventeen years of clerical rule have generally exhibited a trend of increasing pragmatism, interrupted by occasional outbursts of radicalism that were manifestations of ongoing ideological, political, and personal power struggles. This pattern has persisted despite changes in personalities, issues, and alignments. As a result, Iran's policies have often been divergent—that is, cautious and pragmatic on some issues (such as economics and relations with some of Iran's neighbors) and radical on others (such as relations with Islamist movements)—and occasionally even contradictory. Overall, the trend toward pragmatism has strengthened, but the power struggle continues.

The co-leadership of pragmatist President Rafsanjani and more radical Supreme Leader Khamene'i has not proved an adequate substitute for Ayatollah Khomeini's authoritative and charismatic rule. Neither man has Khomeini's religious authority, political power, mass appeal, or personal charisma. Relations between the two have fluctuated between cooperation and competition. They have at times publicly supported each other and cooperated against the regime's opponents, and at other times competed for power and promoted distinctly different views and priorities. Yet both men realize that they must coordinate, consult, or at least inform each other before making crucial decisions. There appears to be an informal division of labor between them, with Rafsanjani taking the lead in economic and foreign policy, and Khamene'i directing moral and spiritual issues, Iran's ties to other Islamist movements, and other spheres.

Rafsanjani has proven to be a shrewd, sophisticated, and successful politician. After eight years as speaker and two terms as president, he has survived the vicissitudes of political change. Despite eroding support for the Islamic regime, he remains personally popular, although his support appears to have declined since he was first elected president in 1989. Many

Iranians apparently continue to believe that his pragmatic approach is the only way to extricate Iran from its economic crisis, but are disappointed that he has thus far failed to demonstrate the necessary determination, persistence, and leadership to achieve many of his stated economic and foreign policy goals.

ECONOMIC DIFFICULTIES

The cumulative legacy of the shah, the regime's own policies, and structural changes in global markets led to a serious decline in the Iranian economy, and this remains the Islamic regime's most pressing challenge. The revolution led to the flight of the professional class (and with it domestic capital) and a sharp drop in foreign investment. The eight-year war with Iraq required costly expenditures, destroyed vital infrastructure, and created growing numbers of refugees.

These pressures were exacerbated by rapid population growth and urbanization, which hampered efforts to provide essential public services such as education, housing, healthcare, basic utilities such as drinking water and electricity, and employment. Iran's reliance on oil revenues to finance post-war reconstruction made it vulnerable to the decline in world oil prices. As imports increased, Tehran fell behind on its debt payments. Inflation put many commodities beyond the reach of ordinary people, while the black market boomed and speculators prospered. Overall, the affluent became wealthier and the gap between rich and poor remains as wide as before the revolution.

The Islamic regime's attempts to remedy these problems became enmeshed in ongoing political disputes. Rafsanjani's reforms—such as increasing privatization, cooperating with international financial institutions, encouraging foreign investment, and similar measures—often caused hardships for the poor and deviated from basic ideological convictions, which infuriated the radicals. A series of corruption and fraud scandals involving senior officials (some of them clerics) in the government, banks, and charitable organizations reinforced popular cynicism toward the government and prompted comparisons between the clerical regime and the reign of the shah. When the government did admit difficulties, it usually blamed middlemen for profiteering, the West for magnifying problems in an attempt to incite popular disaffection, and radicals for hindering efforts to remedy the situation. Despite pledges to the contrary, it has failed to improve the lives of the poor, and the resultant economic decay threatens the political stability of the Islamic Republic.

POPULAR OPPOSITION AND THE GOVERNMENT'S RESPONSE

Although the Islamic Republic has allowed criticism of its economic policies and corruption, the apparent intensity of public debate should not be mistaken for genuine freedom of expression. The scope of permissible dissent or criticism is extremely narrow and limited to partisans of the ruling movement. The government uses harsh measures—from threats and harassment to censorship, arrest and imprisonment, and instigation and tolerance of mob violence—against domestic opponents and critics who transgress those limits. At the same time, popular discontent in the 1990s has increasingly been expressed through strikes, assassination attempts on officials (including Rafsanjani and Khamene'i), bombings (often resulting in heavy casualties) and occasional riots in which many people were killed and arrested, and some later executed. Although the government has blamed the incidents on anti-social elements and foreign conspiracies aimed at turning public opinion against the government, it is genuinely concerned by the popular nature of the uprisings, the fact that the grievances touched upon some basic failures of the government, and that the target of their attacks embraced key symbols of the regime.

Similarly worrisome to the government was the security forces' initially slow and ineffective response to the disturbances, which raised questions about the loyalty of the armed forces. There were already rumblings of discontent within the armed forces due to low salaries and economic hardships. The army has made clear that it will not shoot Iranians in the streets. The government was eventually forced to set up special rapid-deployment anti-riot forces to combat domestic unrest.

IRAN'S REGIONAL AND FOREIGN POLICY

In addition to major domestic developments, unprecedented regional events and trends combined to redefine Iran's regional stature and foreign policy in the 1990s, and present it with both new opportunities and serious challenges. The disintegration of the Soviet Union removed Iran's traditional threat from the north and led to the emergence of six independent Muslim republics close to its borders. The 1991 Gulf War considerably weakened Iraq and stimulated a renewed Iranian drive for regional hegemony in the Gulf and beyond. The post-Gulf War Arab-Israeli peace process (and the participation therein by Syria) further isolated Iran, but also represented one of the rare issues in which its ideology and national interests (as perceived by the ruling elite) converge, and thus provided Tehran with an opportunity to demonstrate regional and Islamic leadership as head of the anti-peace axis.

Islamist movements view the Iranian revolution as a successful model of the ability of the people, led by clerics and inspired by Islam, to topple a regime with a powerful army and the support of a superpower. Tehran has encouraged the growth of Islamism by providing guidance and political and financial support for various Islamist movements, particularly those actively opposed to the peace process. But local regimes and foreign powers have also learned that lesson of the Islamic revolution. They are now more aware of the Islamist challenge and more determined to confront it—and the outside world is more tolerant of the use of oppressive measures to do so. Thus, while the revolution encouraged other Islamist movements, it also created significant barriers to their success.

Animosity toward the United States—a major tenet of the revolution which remains strong under the Islamic regime—has fueled broad opposition from radicals and conservatives (including Khamene'i) to the pragmatists' calls for better relations with Washington. Despite this, and the U.S. dual containment policy (which has not been strictly imposed by the United States itself and lacks the support of U.S. allies), economic ties between the two countries actually expanded until 1995, when Washington banned all trade with Iran. Critics dismiss the idea that trade sanctions can either transform or bring down the Islamic government, arguing that they could instead strengthen the radicals by discrediting the pragmatists.

Yet the European alternative to dual containment—known as "critical dialogue"—has failed to produce significant results. Western countries' concerns about Iran's arms build-up, support for radical Islamist movements, and abuse of human rights have been mitigated by their other interests. Moreover, an economically stronger Iran has little incentive to discard its radical ideology. Though Washington remains willing to engage in a dialogue with authorized Iranian representatives, the Islamic Republic's challenge to the region is likely to persist as long as it retains its present ideological tenets. The problem is not whether Rafsanjani and his supporters seek a change, but the degree to which they are capable of leading Iran to it.

Abbreviations of Sources

AFP	Agence France Presse
DR	Foreign Broadcast Information Service *Daily Report* (Middle East)
EIU	Economist Intelligence Unit
FT	*Financial Times*
IHT	*International Herald Tribune*
IJMES	*International Journal of Middle East Studies*
IRNA	Islamic Revolution News Agency (Tehran)
IT	*Iran Times* (Washington)
JI	*Jomhuri-ye Islami* (Tehran)
JP	*Jerusalem Post*
JPRS	Joint Publication Research Services
KH	*Kayhan Hava'i* (Tehran)
KI	*Kayhan International* (Tehran)
LAT	*Los Angeles Times*
MECS	*Middle East Contemporary Survey*
MEED	*Middle East Economic Digest*
MEJ	*Middle East Journal*
NYT	*New York Times*
SWB	*Summary of World Broadcasting* (British Broadcasting Corp.)
TT	*Tehran Times*

I

Introduction:
The Framework of Iranian Politics

The 1979 Islamic revolution in Iran presents a new pattern of power-seizure in the modern history of the Middle East. Typically, the many *coups* in this region in the last generation were carried out by small groups led mostly by army officers, who only after their seizure of power sought popular support for themselves and their new ideology. The Iranian revolution was a striking exception: It was led primarily by clerics, enjoyed popular support not as a consequence of but as a prerequisite for seizing power, and its "new" ideology was nothing more than the return to the glorious past and ideology most familiar to Iranians—Islam.

For all the salient differences distinguishing it from other Middle Eastern *coups,* the Islamic revolution was nevertheless consistent with earlier opposition movements in modern Iran. Three similar outbursts in the last century are noteworthy. The Tobacco Movement (1891-92) rallied against the tobacco concession (and capitulations system in general) and forced the shah to revoke the concession; the Constitutional Revolution (1905-11) forced the shah to approve a constitution that limited his power; and the national movement headed by Mohammad Mosaddeq (prime minister, 1951-53) forced the shah into temporary exile.

The Islamic revolution shares certain common characteristics with these earlier movements. Each began in reaction to the reigning shah's policies, which were injurious to various socio-economic groups and caused diverse forces to unite around common causes. In all but the Mosaddeq movement, the clerics were the main driving force and amply proved their ability to mobilize mass support. Mass action played a major and even decisive role in each. Mounting social and economic tensions, intensified autocratic rule, growing secularization, and extensive foreign influence were pivotal in the events leading up to them. And, notwithstanding their differences, in all four movements various groups rallied around a powerful, unifying symbol: tobacco in the late nineteenth century; constitutionalism in the early twentieth century; nationalism, oil, or nationalization of oil in the 1950s; and Islam in the late 1970s.

All four movements succeeded in attaining their initial goals. But whereas the earlier eruptions had limited objectives (i.e., to change one major item on the government's agenda), the Islamic revolution sought to change the regime itself. To its leaders, "Islamic revolution" was not merely a title for a movement, nor intended for Iran alone. It was an ideal they wished to put into practice throughout the Muslim world, with Iran as the starting point. It contained the desire to solve the problems facing the population, thereby creating an ideal Islamic order and turning Iran into a model for other Islamic communities to imitate: a *revolution* in all spheres of life, *Islamic* in character and orientation.

For the first seventeen years of their rule, the clerics concentrated on two main targets: the consolidation, institutionalization, and (as far as possible) perpetuation of their rule; and more importantly, the implementation of Ayatollah Ruhollah Khomeini's revolutionary ideology, which would advance the country and in turn further promote its own legitimization and consolidation.

Since the initial two years or so of clerical rule, the Islamic regime has demonstrated a measure of political stability. As was the case throughout Iran's constitutional history, the duration in office of individual governments seems a valid yardstick of such a stability. In the four years that began with the autumn 1977 revolutionary crisis that eventually led to the overthrow of the shah, there were ten prime ministers (five between February 1979 and October 1981 alone); between January 1980 and October 1981, there were three presidential elections.

By contrast, between October 1981 and the summer of 1989, Iran had the same president ('Ali Khamene'i), Majlis speaker ('Ali Akbar Hashemi Rafsanjani), prime minister (Mir-Hosein Musavi), president of the supreme court ('Abdul-Karim Ardebili), and the same supreme religious and political leader (*rahbar*), Khomeini.[1] Moreover, his death in June 1989 was similarly marked by stability and continuity. Khamenc'i became the *rahbar* and Rafsanjani replaced him as president (with the position of the prime minister being abolished). Majlis and presidential elections have been held on schedule every four years since.

Though fairly successful in stabilizing its control, the clerical regime has thus far proven less effective in implementing Islam as a vehicle to resolve the mounting social, economic and political problems that led to the revolution in the first place.[2] This has become the Islamic regime's main challenge in the 1990s.

In properly comprehending the profound changes in Iran after the revolution, three issues are particularly pertinent:

• *The extent to which the Iranian revolution (and similar Islamist movements) are truly religious in their roots and goals.* Islam encompasses all spheres of life, making no distinctions between religion, politics, science, *et cetera*. Thus, from an Islamic perspective, the economic distress, social disparities, political repression, foreign exploitation, and rapid modernization that served as the catalysts for the revolution are inherently "religious." In

---

[1]   For a more detailed explanation of the position of *rahbar*, see footnote 1 in Chapter II.

[2]   For a discussion of their initial success in consolidating their rule, see Menashri, "The Islamic Revolution in Iran: The Consolidation Phase," *Orient*, April 1984, pp. 499-515; and Menashri, *Iran: A Decade of War and Revolution* (New York: Holmes and Meier, 1990), pp. 4-11.

Western terms, however, the roots and goals of the Islamic revolution extend far beyond religion. In fact, Iranians rose against the shah for a variety of reasons, and saw Islam as the vehicle to end societal malaise and provide their children with a better life. Thus, the stabilization of the new regime depends less on the degree of its return to Islam than the degree to which it solves or at least eases the problems that initially fueled popular discontent. Though public expectations went far beyond the Western notion of "religious" issues, the overthrow of the shah led to the creation of an Islamic regime and in that sense was undeniably an *Islamic revolution.*

• *Whether the doctrine of Khomeini—who came to be identified in the West with Islam (or at least Shi'ism)—represented traditional Islam or a departure from conservative Islamic thought.* If early Islam is the yardstick, Khomeini's vision was in many respects conservative; but if "tradition" refers to the theories and practices of the last centuries of Islamic thought, Khomeini's vision was more innovative and revolutionary than traditional.[3] In fact, in ideological terms, Khomeini's doctrine represents a revolution in recent Islamic thought no less than an Islamic revolution.

• *The degree to which the Islamic regime remained loyal to its dogma after the transition from opposition to power.* Much like other ideological movements, upon assuming power and facing the complex demands of governance, the new regime was to some degree forced to adapt itself to new realities. In opposition, they could advance a theoretical model of the ideal Islamic state; once in power, however, they could not govern by revolutionary slogans. Obliged to manage rather than theorize about affairs of state, they had to make compromises, not from a new-found moderation, but in a pragmatic response to the exigencies of their situation. Yet in terms of specific areas of policy and the degree and rate of change, the various factions differed widely. Iranian policies thus remained divergent and often contradictory.

One reason for these apparent contradictions is perhaps the difficulty of simultaneously assimilating momentous domestic changes and the series of regional upheavals that began buffeting the Middle East in the late 1980s. The combination presented both new opportunities and serious challenges and dilemmas.

Domestically, three main challenges evolved:

• *The death of Khomeini* in 1989 ended his all-powerful, charismatic style of leadership and called into question the essence of the religio-political guardianship (*marja'iyya*) of the revolution.

• *The resultant struggle for power and the emergence of the Rafsanjani-Khamene'i co-leadership* has yet to prove an adequate substitute for Khomeini's authoritative and charismatic rule. Neither has his religious authority,

---

[3] Nikki Keddie, "Iran: Change in Islam, Islam in Change," *IJMES* 2 (1980), p. 532. See also Hava Lazarus-Yaffe, "Ha-Shi'a be-torato ha-politit shel Khomeini" (Shi'ism in Khomeini's Political Thought), *Ha-Mizrah Ha-Hadash* 30 (1982), pp. 99-106.

political power, mass appeal, or personal charisma. Khomeini's most important (and sometimes painful) decisions remained beyond argument; those of the current leadership do not. Overall, Rafsanjani's pragmatist faction seemed to have strengthened its position, but the power struggle continued on two levels: an open conflict between Rafsanjani and his radical and conservative rivals, and a more latent and personal struggle between Rafsanjani and Khamene'i themselves. And even when they agree, they are often confronted by more radical and conservative factions.

• *Growing social and economic difficulties* have given rise to sharp popular dissatisfaction and marked disillusionment. This has resulted in greater realism in the government and an emphasis on "reasons of the state" over the initial "ideological crusade."[4] Yet even this has not helped to ease—let alone solve—the difficulties facing the *mostaz'afin* (dispossessed).

At the same time, unprecedented regional developments had direct influence on Iranian policy:

• *The disintegration of the Soviet Union* removed Iran's traditional threat from the north and led to the emergence of six Islamic republics close to its borders, thus creating new opportunities to advance Iranian regional ambitions. The fall of the "Islamic iron curtain"[5] also made it possible for Iran (at least in its own view) to open a new chapter in its relations with Russia as more equal powers. Moreover, Iran saw the need for the Muslim and/or developing worlds to fill the vacuum created by the demise of the USSR, and wished to be the leading element in such an effort. But the change also posed significant challenges and dilemmas for Tehran, such as the need to preserve regional stability, limit the influence of unfriendly countries competing for sway in the Muslim regions of the former USSR, and prevent the possible infiltration into Iran of ideological influences from newly-independent republics such as Azerbaijan.

• *The 1991 Gulf War* considerably weakened (at least temporarily) Iran's major rival, Iraq; led to tensions between its Arab neighbors (Iraq versus Saudi Arabia and Kuwait); and stimulated a renewed Iranian drive for regional hegemony in the Gulf and beyond.

• *The Arab-Israeli peace process*—and the participation therein by Iran's main Arab ally, Syria—further isolated Tehran as the leader of the anti-peace axis. Having made Palestine a major issue on its foreign policy agenda, Tehran was now willing (or felt obliged) to offer its leadership to this camp. Though this provided an avenue to demonstrate regional and Islamic centrality, it also presented significant dilemmas and potentially serious challenges.

• *The growth of Islamism,* largely inspired by Iran and to which it was deeply committed, has similarly required Tehran to provide patronage,

---

[4] R. K. Ramazani, "Iran's Foreign Policy: Both North and South," *Middle East Journal* 46, no. 3 (summer 1992), p. 395.

[5] Shireen T. Hunter, "The Emergence of Soviet Muslims: Impact on the Middle East," *Middle East Insight* 8, no. 5 (May-June 1992), p. 32.

support, and guardianship in order to establish its leadership of the Muslim communities. This also presented new opportunities to strengthen and expand its regional and ideological influence, but once again significant challenges such as growing tension with regional states quickly became evident.

Some scholars viewed Khomeini's death as the beginning of the "second republic."[6] Others viewed the fall of the USSR as ushering in "the second phase" of Iranian foreign policy.[7] The *Iran Times* went as far as to suggest that the "world turned upside down."[8] Although the revolutionary nature of such changes is beyond argument, their combined impact did not necessarily generate a clear-cut policy. They have at times led to ambiguity, dualism, and even contradictions. This paper seeks to analyze internal developments and examine their influence on Iran's policy and posture.

[6] See Anoushirvan Ehteshami, *After Khomeini: The Iranian Second Republic* (London: Routledge, 1995).

[7] See editorial in *Hamshahri*, February 9, in *DR*, February 23, 1993.

[8] *IT*, October 1, 1993.

II

The Guardianship of the Jurisconsult: Failure of a Dogma

Perhaps the most profound achievement of the 1979 Islamic revolution was the unification of religion and state, and with it the transfer of all power—theological and mundane—to the highest religious authority: the *marja'-e taqlid* (source of imitation) or, as the concept is known in the parlance of the revolution, *velayat-e faqih* (guardianship or vice regency of the jurisconsult).[1] Yet it was also in this realm that Khomeini's disciples faced their most crucial ideological challenge. The problem consisted of two interrelated elements. First, there was the ideological conflict between the philosophy of the revolution (which held that leadership should be entrusted to a prominent cleric and defined the limits of government authority under Islamic rule) and the interests of the Iranian state. Second, there were factional and personal conflicts regarding issues of politics, succession, the power structure, and the struggle for power. In a clear deviation from the creed of the revolution, the regime was forced to give greater weight to political considerations, and power gradually moved from theologians to religio-politicians who emphasized Iran's national interests (or those of the regime in power) over Islamic doctrine.[2]

KHOMEINI'S ENDORSEMENT OF RETREAT FROM DOCTRINE

Khomeini himself often intervened to sanction the authority of the religio-politicians at the expense of prominent clerics. Under the

---

[1] The 1979 Iranian constitution (Articles 5, 107, and 112) vests paramount religious and political authority in a supreme "Leader" (*rahbar*)—a position unparalleled in Iran's earlier constitutional history but consistent with the concept of *velayat-e faqih*. The Leader (among others) is responsible for "delineating the general policies" of the state and "supervising the execution of those policies" (Article 110). Amendments to the constitution after Khomeini's death in 1989 no longer required candidates to be a *marja'* (one of the supreme religious authorities), thereby allowing any *mojtahed* (jurist with the "scholastic qualifications for issuing religious decrees") to be Leader. For a discussion of the 1979 constitution, see Menashri, *A Decade of War and Revolution* (New York: Holmes and Meier, 1990), pp. 116-26; on the amendments, see *MECS* 1989, pp. 348-49.

[2] The distinction between theologians and "religio-politicians" is complex. Leading politicians such as Rafsanjani have religious credentials, and eminent clerics often engage in politics. In the context of this discussion, persons who gained prominence on the basis of their religious scholarship and authority are deemed theologians, whereas those who exercise authority as a result of their political power are referred to as religio-politicians.

constitution, for example, the twelve-man Council of Guardians (Shura-ye Negahban), which is comprised of six clerics appointed by Khomeini and six jurists chosen by the Majlis, is charged with reviewing laws passed by the Majlis to determine whether they are in conformity with Islamic law and compatible with the constitution. Due to its conservative Islamic approach, the Council vetoed many laws that the government deemed essential to its aims (e.g., redistribution of land, nationalizing foreign trade, taxation, and labor practices), to the point of obstructing government functions.[3]

Khomeini pressured the Council to reverse itself and approve laws it had previously vetoed. In a series of notes he exchanged with Khamene'i and the Council in December 1987 and January 1988, he elaborated on one of the principal questions in Shi'i theology: the limits of government power.[4] His ruling was an important step in stripping the Council of its exclusive constitutional authority. At the same time, he even sanctioned the Islamic state's authority to "destroy a mosque" or suspend the exercise of the "five pillars of faith" if state interest (*selah-e keshvar*) so required.[5]

A month later he went a step further. In response to an appeal by a group of prominent officials who sought to bypass the Council in case of a disagreement with the Majlis, Khomeini decreed that such an impasse should be resolved by an assembly consisting of the six theologian members of the Council of Guardians and six state officials: the president, prime minister, Majlis speaker, president of the supreme court, prosecutor general, and the minister concerned with the proposed legislation. The assembly's decision, he decreed, "must be accepted."[6] This represented another blatant retreat from his own doctrine. The authority to determine the state's interest[7] was thus entrusted to a mixed assembly (i.e., comprised of theologians, religio-politicians, and government officials with no Islamic training), thereby depriving the Council of Guardians of its exclusive right to approve legislation. In August 1988, Khomeini ordered the formation of a four-man council (the Shura-ye Ta'yin-e Siyasatha-ye Bazsazi) comprised of the heads of the three branches of government (Rafsanjani, Khamene'i and Ardebili) and the prime minister (Musavi) to resolve disagreements over post-war reconstruction policy and ministerial appointments.[8]

Through these steps, Khomeini in fact sanctioned the supremacy of the state over the philosophy of the revolution, which was whittled down in the face of harsh realities. Such a decision "in favor of state paramountcy

---

[3] On the constitutional authority of the Council, see Menashri, *A Decade of War and Revolution*, pp. 117, 192-93. On the use of such power to block radical legislation, see pp. 173, 183, 224, 246, 327-28, and 356-58.

[4] The decrees are cited in *Ettela'at*, January 7 and 12, 1988.

[5] *Kayhan* (Tehran), January 7, 1988.

[6] *Ettela'at*, February 7, 1988.

[7] This phrase was incorporated into the name of the new body, the Shura-ye Tashkhis-e Maslahat (roughly, the Discretionary Council).

[8] *Ettela'at*, August 31, 1988.

in society's affairs" gave "dramatic new power to the state," sanctioned its dominance over society,[9] and even "permitted the state to violate citizens' rights for common good."[10] As Rafsanjani interpreted Khomeini's guidelines, "The law should follow Islamic doctrine. However, if necessary, priority will be given to government decision over doctrine."[11] This was a serious blow to the most basic doctrine of the revolution.

THE POLITICS OF SUCCESSION

Khomeini's succession prompted another blatant deviation from the concept of *velayat-e faqih*. Given the prominence of the *vali faqih* in the Islamic regime, it was crucial to guarantee a smooth transfer of power from one to another. According to Shi'i tradition (now embodied in the Islamic regime and the 1979 Iranian constitution), he is supposed to be the most learned and righteous *faqih* (*a'lam va asdaq*). It soon became evident, however, that these criteria were (as Mehdi Bazargan once said) "a garment fit only for Mr. Khomeini."[12] None of the leading theologians of the rank of *ayatollah 'uzma* (grand ayatollah) fully accepted Khomeini's doctrine, and none of his followers had his prominent religious standing (not to mention his charisma and political authority).

There were numerous instances in Shi'i history in which no single *faqih* was accepted as the sole source of authority, and the result was often a kind of collective spiritual leadership in which, as Khomeini himself pointed out, there was a continuing debate over theological issues among senior clerics.[13] Major Shi'i thinkers have even argued that having a single *marja'* (guide) "ran counter to the principles of Shi'ism."[14] In the past, these ideological differences had "existed [only] in books."[15] Now, given the civil power the clerics had assumed, their disputes could—and did—disrupt the effective administration of the government. The fact that they now wielded complete power made the selection of a (single) successor essential.

Yet the leading theologians of 1979 were either resentful of the *velayat-e faqih* concept as practiced by the ruling clerics (as was the case for Kazem Shari'atmadari, 'Abdollah Shirazi, and eventually Abul-Qasem Kho'i) or

---

[9] Farhad Kazemi, "Civil Society and Iranian Politics," in *Civil Society in the Middle East*, vol. 2, ed. Augustus R. Norton (Leiden, The Netherlands: Brill, 1996), pp. 123-24.

[10] Ervand Abrahamian, *Khomeinism: Essays on the Islamic Republic* (Berkeley, CA: University of California Press, 1993), p. 57. See also Ahmad Ashraf, "Theocracy and Charisma: New Men of Power in Iran," *International Journal of Politics, Culture, and Society* 4 (1990), p. 139.

[11] NHK Television (Tokyo), February 1, in *SWB*, February 3, 1988.

[12] *Middle East Policy* 3, no. 4 (1995), p. 26.

[13] *JI*, November 7; *Kayhan* (Tehran), November 26, 1988.

[14] Laurent Lamote [pseudonym], "Domestic Politics and Strategic Intentions," in *Iran's Strategic Intentions and Capabilities*, ed. Patrick Clawson (Washington, DC: National Defense University, 1994), pp. 10-12.

[15] Khamene'i on Radio Tehran, November 11, in *SWB*, November 14, 1988.

distanced themselves from daily politics (as was the case with Seyyed Shihab al-Din Najafi-Mar'ashi, Mohammad Reza Golpaygani and Mohammad 'Ali Araki). Some vehemently opposed Khomeini's doctrine and were forcibly silenced, others were less vocal or acknowledged his power and gave their blessing to the facts he or his disciples established. In a way, Khomeini's doctrine constituted a revolution in recent Shi'i Islamic political thought no less than an Islamic revolution. He introduced new interpretations and gained support for them mainly from low-ranking clerics or religio-politicians over the heads of the senior theologians.

The succession issue presented the regime with a theological challenge and political obstacle. The most prominent theologians were not politically suited for succession, and the religio-politicians lacked the proper religious credentials. To avoid a succession crisis, Khomeini and his disciples first "promoted" Ayatollah Hosein 'Ali Montazeri to the rank of *ayatollah 'uzma* at the outset of the revolution and then officially selected him as heir apparent in 1985. In 1987, Khomeini also revised his will, apparently to avoid a posthumous succession struggle. Although the selection of Montazeri defied traditional practice and Khomeini's own creed (since there were greater religious authorities still alive)—and had more to do with Montazeri's role in the revolution than pure scholarship or piety, he nonetheless had significant religious credentials. Yet despite the fact that loyalty was an essential element in his selection, Montazeri's subsequent criticisms of the government led to his disqualification in March 1989—another example of the supremacy of political considerations.

Given Khomeini's failing health, changes to the constitution were essential to further adapt the doctrine of the revolution to political reality.[16] A series of constitutional amendments in 1989 gave an official blessing to the eventual separation of the positions of *marja'iyya* and *velayat* and thereby allowed any *faqih* (jurist) with "scholastic qualifications for issuing religious decrees" to assume the position of Supreme Leader (Articles 5 and 107). The 1979 stipulation (Article 5) that the Supreme Leader be "recognized and accepted" by "the majority of the people" (a requirement for the *marja'iyya*) was dropped. At the same time, the new constitution stressed that preference be given to those better versed in "political and social issues" (Article 107). While the level of religious scholarship was lowered, political experience was given greater weight—another step in the retreat from dogma.

The selection of Khamene'i (then only *hojjat ul-Islam*, a lower ranking than *ayatollah*) as Supreme Leader, and the subsequent smooth transfer of authority, were undeniable signs of political stability.[17] Yet these were also additional evidence of the failure of doctrine and the ideological impasse facing the regime. Although clerics (albeit of lesser ranks) were still in

---

[16] Khomeini actually died before the constitutional amendment body made its final decisions.

[17] Khamene'i was thereafter referred to as an *ayatollah.*

charge, ultimate authority was no longer exercised by the supreme religious source or even by a prominent theologian. Khamene'i had neither emerged by popular consensus nor received the support of the leading authorities for his religious credentials, but was in fact "promoted" to successor by the religio-politicians.

Having entrusted the leadership to Khamene'i, the regime rallied behind Ayatollah Araki (who was roughly 100 years old and in failing health) as the ideal choice for *marja'*. Araki possessed adequate religious credentials, was likely to support the government but unlikely to usurp power, and would probably not live long. This would give the regime a free hand to pursue its policies with Araki's automatic blessing, while paving the way for Khamene'i to claim the *marja'iyya* in the near future—again a move of political maneuvering more than theological sincerity. Thus, it is not surprising that the regime failed to gain significant support from the public or in clerical circles even for this change. In the end, it was simply easier for the regime to silence prominent authorities who opposed Khomeini's doctrine than to rally support for his hand-picked successor.

The selection of Khamene'i to succeed Khomeini and the eventual separation of *marja'iyya* from *velayat* constituted a fatal blow to the revolution's most basic ideological creed and a blatant retreat from its most significant achievement. If the Islamic government had its origins in the spiritual leadership of the *marja'*, the appointment of Khamene'i demonstrated that "not only individuals but also ideas had played musical chairs"; after all, Khamene'i had never been considered a "doctor of law" (*mujtahid*) qualified to give an independent opinion.[18] No *mullah*, religious student, or even ordinary Iranian "would seek . . . a *fatwa* [religious judgment]" from him.[19] The result was a "divorce" of the supreme religious function from the highest political function: the concept of *velayat-e faqih* "is defunct, but it is too late to go [back] to the old system."[20]

Official attempts to justify the selection of Khamene'i made the enduring gap between ideology and reality even more strikingly evident. Rafsanjani and others claimed that Khomeini had expressed the initial idea of separating the *marj'iyya* and *vilaya* "in private discussions" before his death. Quoting from an April 1989 letter from Khomeini to Ayatollah 'Ali Meshkini, head of the Council of Experts, he added: "Since the very beginning," Khomeini had "insisted" that *marja'iyya* was not a necessary condition for leadership and that any *faqih* (who was not even a *mujtahid*) could be *vali*.[21] Moreover, they now claimed that Khomeini had approved

---

[18] Roy P. Mottahedeh, "The Islamic Movement: The Case of Democratic Inclusion," *Contention* 4, no. 3 (spring 1995), pp. 114-15.

[19] Edward G. Shirley [pseudonym], "Fundamentalism in Power: Is Iran's Present Algeria's Future?" *Foreign Affairs* 74, no. 3 (May-June 1995), p. 38.

[20] Olivier Roy, *The Failure of Political Islam* (Cambridge, MA: Harvard University Press, 1994), p. 179.

[21] Radio Tehran, June 9, in *SWB*, June 12, 1989; *Kayhan* (Tehran), June 11, 1989.

the selection of Khamene'i in advance as his preferred candidate.[22] Conspicuously, the attribution of such ideas and intentions to Khomeini was a blatant refutation of his last will and testament and thus carried no legal weight.[23] They irrefutably ran contrary to his writings and statements since the late 1960s.

Eager to stress Khamene'i's qualifications, officials raised further arguments that wildly contradicted Khomeini's creed. Although the latter had endorsed rule by a prominent cleric, they now placed greater emphasis on political and administrative qualifications than scholarship. "Familiarity with national issues," Rafsanjani said, is "far more important" than knowledge and piety. Khamene'i has eight years experience as president, he noted. "If we selected a Supreme Leader from a seminary, by the time he became familiar with national issues," Iran could "suffer irreparable harm."[24] Ayatollah Ahmad Jannati opined that political shrewdness was the most important quality for the *marja'*.[25] Ayatollah Meshkini observed that prominent clerics were not automatically qualified for leadership, since they lack sufficient knowledge of world conditions "and the political, social, and cultural issues facing Muslims."[26] These were "obvious reference to Khamene'i and a complete reversal of 150 years of Shi'a tradition."[27] In fact, taken only one step further, such arguments would countenance rule by most of the leaders of Muslim states (whom Khomeini did not regard as qualified to govern) since each could claim significant political credentials.

Thus, the interpretations of those holding power were made to appear as Khomeini's views, and their candidate assumed leadership. Since then, the religio-politicians have pursued their own agenda but have sought to achieve a *modus vivendi* with the leading clerics, who more often than not have given government policy their perfunctory blessing.

---

[22] For example, Rafsanjani said that in a meeting with Khomeini, the heads of the three branches of government expressed their concern that the (old) constitution's stipulations regarding his successor might lead to a political vacuum. Khomeini said this was unlikely "since we have the appropriate people for the position. When we asked whom, he pointed to Khamene'i"; see Radio Tehran, June 9, in *SWB*, June 12, 1989. Ayatollah 'Abdul-Qasem Khaz'ali (a member of the Council of Guardians) added that shortly before his death, Khomeini indicated three times that he viewed Khamene'i as the most appropriate successor; see *Resalat* in *DR*, June 5, 1989.

[23] Arguments based on what Khomeini may have said in private bear no legal weight, because his last will explicitly warned that no views attributed to him should be given credence "unless I said it in my own voice [i.e., on tape] or it has my signature [on it, verified by] the affirmation of the experts, or what I said on the television of the Islamic Republic"; see *Imam Khomeini's Last Will and Testament* (Washington, DC: Interest Section of the Islamic Republic of Iran, Algerian Embassy, 1989), p. 62.

[24] *Kayhan* (Tehran), June 10, 1989; Radio Tehran, June 9, in *SWB*, June 12, 1989.

[25] Mottahedeh, pp. 114-15.

[26] IRNA, June 16, in *SWB*, June 19, 1989.

[27] Mottahedeh, pp. 114-15.

The deaths of three prominent authorities—Kho'i in August 1992, Golpaygani in December 1993, and Araki in December 1994—forced a further reckoning with reality and distancing from doctrine. Yet the same succession problem remained: if senior clerics were chosen for *marja'iyya* from outside the political structure, they could challenge it; if they were chosen by those in power, religion would be subordinated to the state and belief subject to the "vicissitudes of politics," thus constituting "a threat to historical Shi'ism."[28]

Signs of clerical opposition to a government-imposed *marja'* became evident after Golpaygani's death.[29] Khamene'i realized that he was unlikely to obtain recognition as the supreme *marja'* in the short term. Aware that he lacked sufficient religious credentials, his associates again emphasized his political qualifications. Khamene'i was already a senior *marja'*, argued Ayatollah Mohammad Yazdi, and therefore his instructions in matters of jurisprudence were already binding. Moreover, Yazdi questioned whether a pious person who lacked the rudiments of political and social experience was even qualified to be the supreme *marja'*, as that implied a separation between religion and politics.[30] Khamene'i was "the most qualified compared to all his peers and equals with regard to his awareness of the requirements of time, management ability, administrative skills," Yazdi argued, and also had the necessary religious credentials. If a pious candidate for supreme *marja'* "fails to understand the most basic social and political issues of the Islamic community," he asked, "should he be the source of emulation?"[31]

Khamene'i failed to muster popular support to be the *marja'*, however, and the regime—while preparing for his next opportunity—rallied again around Araki.[32] The Qom Theological Lecturers Association (Jame'-ye Modarresin-e Qom) stated that the "source of imitation" was henceforth embodied in Araki,[33] and Ayatollah Mohammad Javadi-Amoli said that the *marja'iyya* of the world's Shi'a "rests today" with him.[34]

But Araki's death came sooner than expected, and well before Khamene'i could significantly enhance his chances. A new round of "electioneering" began, with establishment figures promoting Khamene'i's candidacy for the *marja'* once again. Having recently failed to gain such recognition, however, they had to be content with his acceptance as one of

---

[28] *IT*, December 24, 1993.

[29] *Al-Sharq al-Awsat* in *IT*, December 31, 1993. Clerics then reportedly signed a letter protesting the regime's efforts to control the selection of the *marja'*; see *IT*, December 24, 1993, and January 7, 1994.

[30] IRNA, December 10, in *DR*, December 12, 1993; *IT*, December 17, 1993.

[31] Radio Tehran, December 17, in *DR*, December 20, 1993; *Salam*, December 18, 1993; *IT*, December 17 and 24, 1993.

[32] *IT*, January 28, 1994.

[33] *Ettela'at*, December 12, 1993; *IT*, December 17, 1993.

[34] Tehran TV, December 25, in *DR*, December 27, 1993.

those possessing *marja'iyya* qualifications. The late Araki was quoted as having given him "generous, decisive, unequivocal and all-embracing support" as the custodian of the affairs of the world's Muslims.[35] Speaker 'Ali Akbar Nateq Nuri[36] and Ayatollah Yazdi[37] presented Khamene'i as the future *marja'*. Yazdi referred to him as "the esteemed leader and fully qualified theologian" in charge of "leading the Muslims on behalf of the lord of the era."[38] His name also appeared on numerous lists of those possessing full qualifications (*jame' al-sharayet*) to serve as *marja'* issued by various organizations, including the Qom Theological Lecturers Association,[39] the Combatant Clergy Association (Jame'-ye Ruhaniyyat-e Mobarez or JRM),[40] and the Combatant Clerics of Tehran (Ruhaniyyun-e Mobarez-e Tehran or RMT).[41] More prominent clerics like Montazeri, Hasan Tabataba'i Qomi, Mohammad Sadeq Ruhani, and Seyyed 'Ali Hoseini Sistani were once again ignored.

DIVISIONS WITHIN THE CLERGY

In addition to decrying Khamene'i's lack of religious qualifications and the fact that greater authorities had been passed over, dissident clerics protested the government's interference in selecting the *marja'* and its politically motivated departure from Islamic doctrine. Mehdi Ha'eri, living in exile in Germany, argued that the regime made its intentions clear after Golpaygani's death by arresting Ayatollah Sadeq Ruhani, who advocated the separation of religion and state, and raiding his residence.[42] In what was purported to be an open letter to the Iranian authorities, Ruhani asked for an exit visa, complaining that life in Iran has become "unbearable for those who abide by the true principles" of Islam. He was quoted as claiming that "armed criminals" had attacked his home in Qom and threatened to kill him unless he declared allegiance to Khamene'i. He added that he could not "remain a spectator while Islam is violated daily" and "true religious leaders" are silenced in a country "claiming to be an Islamic Republic."[43] In July 1995, a group of armed men again attacked Ruhani's residence. A statement by Hojjat ul-Islam Gholam-Hosein Rahimi called the attackers messengers of the "*taghut* [idol-worshipping] regime,"

---

[35] Ibid., December 1, in *DR*, December 2, 1994.

[36] Ibid., December 3, in *DR*, December 5, 1994.

[37] Radio Tehran, December 9, in *DR*, December 12, 1994.

[38] Tehran TV, November 30, in *DR*, November 30, 1994.

[39] Ibid., December 2, in *DR*, December 5, 1994.

[40] IRNA, December 2, in *DR*, December 5, 1994.

[41] Radio Tehran, December 9, in *DR*, December 12, 1994.

[42] *IT*, January 7, 1994. IRNA (January 5, 1994) quoted Ruhani's son's denial of this report; see *DR*, January 5, 1994.

[43] *Al-Sharq al-Awsat*, January 25, 1995.

a term normally used to refer to the shah's government. Ruhani's followers called for the release of his son Javad and other supporters, whose sole crime was following a legitimate *marja'*. Several other clerics joined the protest in Iran, as did Ruhani's brother, Mehdi Ruhani, who lived in exile in Paris.[44]

Government officials denied that the recognition of the new *marja'* represented any challenge to the Islamic establishment. Khamene'i said that the West had found a handful of "illiterate . . . pseudo-clerics" and supplied them with money and microphones. They were aiming, he said, to "undermine the lofty and divine status" of the *marja'iyya* and insinuate that the public had turned their backs on the clergy.[45] Nateq Nuri referred to them as the "Sultans' preachers" (*vo'az ul-salatin*) and "court clerics" (*akhundha-ye darbari*) who had fled Iran because of their black record.[46] Rafsanjani dismissed the whole issue as Zionist-imperialist propaganda and the "most basic form of [Western] cultural onslaught."[47]

As in the past, any developments relating to the *marja'iyya* were linked to the disqualification of Montazeri.[48] Yet he was not the first *ayatollah* whose status was affected by political consideration, just as Ruhani was not the first to be forcibly silenced. In the early days of the revolution, Ayatollah Kazem Shari'atmadari was intimidated into silence by recurrent verbal and physical assaults on his home and followers. In 1982, he was accused of having supported a plot against the regime. The JRM then announced that he was not qualified to be a *marja'*[49] or recognized as a grand *ayatollah*.[50] Demonstrators demanded that he be stripped of his religious title; some even called for his execution.[51]

After his disqualification, Montazeri was often accused of opposing government policy and his activities were closely monitored. He still posed a challenge to the regime, mostly on an ideological level, but with political implications as well. He had many supporters, and his lectures—in which he allegedly criticized the government—incurred the authorities' anger. In

---

[44] In September 1995, Javad Ruhani was sentenced to three years in prison; see Israel Radio (Persian Service), August 5-12 and September 16, 1995; and *Kayhan* (London), July 27, in *DR*, September 13, 1995.

[45] Radio Tehran, December 14, in *DR*, December 15, 1994.

[46] Ibid., December 3, in *DR*, December 5, 1994.

[47] Ibid., December 30, in *DR*, December 30, 1994. See similar statement in this context by Khamene'i, ibid., December 14, in *DR*, December 15, 1994.

[48] For more on his nomination, see David Menashri, "Iran," in *MECS* 1984-85, pp. 433-35; on his dismissal, see *MECS* 1989, pp. 341-44.

[49] Radio Tehran, April 21, in *DR*, April 22, 1982. Among the signatories were Rafsanjani, Khamene'i, Musavi, Nateq Nuri, Ardebili, and Mahdavi-Kani. For the rivalries between Shari'atmadari and Khomeini, see Menashri, "Shi'ite Leadership: In the Shadow of Conflicting Ideologies," *Iranian Studies* 3, nos. 1-4 (1980), pp. 119-45; and Menashri, *A Decade of War and Revolution*, pp. 82-90, 129-30, 224-25, 239-40.

[50] *Ettela'at*, April 22, 24, 26, 1982; *JI*, April 22, 1982; *TT*, May 1, 1982.

[51] *The Guardian*, April 22, 1982.

February 1993, for example, he decried the amount of money that was spent to celebrate the anniversary of the revolution. He portrayed himself as the "midwife" of the revolution and of its "wet nurses" and criticized the ruling clerics for usurping his right of succession.[52] In response, government supporters marched to his house chanting pro-regime and anti-Montazeri slogans. The demonstration soon developed into a violent clash.[53] *Jomhuri-ye Islami* described Montazeri as simpleminded and influenced by satanic forces, and threatened to publish a 1989 letter by Khomeini that it claimed was critical of Montazeri and would lead people to "realize their duty."[54] Opposition sources claimed that Montazeri and some of his associates had been detained and that five had been executed.[55]

In March 1993, anti-Montazeri elements distributed a copy of a letter he had allegedly written to Golpaygani protesting against low-ranking clerics taking control of the revolution. In an October 1994 statement, Montazeri condemned the monopolization of the revolution by "a certain group," blamed the authorities for having deviated from the path of the revolution, and criticized injustice toward and the lack of security for the public.[56] Nine clerics close to him were reportedly arrested on charges of instigating sedition by distributing his statement.[57] Two months later, pro-government students demonstrated outside his house, shouting slogans against him and demanding the suspension of his classes.[58]

Although the authenticity of letters attributed to Montazeri remains in question, his charges touched upon sensitive issues: religious qualifications required for leadership (implying criticism of Khamene'i) and mishandling the affairs of the state (implying criticism of Rafsanjani). That Montazeri "stands apart" from the regime and continues to entertain political ambitions concerns the regime. The government's response to his charges indicates "extreme sensitivity to any challenge" to Khamene'i's authority.[59] It is therefore not surprising that a November 1991 visit by a group of some eighty Majlis deputies to Montazeri in Qom turned into a major political incident.[60] *Resalat*, suggesting that the radicals may have been behind the release of the alleged Montazeri letter in March 1993, criticized them and called upon the radical newspaper *Salam* to clarify its

---

[52] *JI*, February 15, 1993.

[53] *Kayhan* (London), February 14 and 18, 1993, in *Echo of Iran*, no. 61 (February 1993), p. 14; *DR*, February 19, 1993.

[54] *JI*, February 15, 1993.

[55] IRNA, February 16, in *DR*, February 17, 1993; *Al-Sharq al-Awsat*, February 16, 1993.

[56] *Kayhan* (London), October 20, in *DR*, December 1, 1994.

[57] *Al-Sharq al-Awsat* (London), November 2, 1994.

[58] AFP, December 26, in *DR*, December 28, 1994.

[59] Shaul Bakhash, "The Crisis of Legitimacy," in *Middle Eastern Lectures* (Tel Aviv: Moshe Dayan Center, 1995), p. 99.

[60] *MECS* 1991, pp. 389-90.

attitude concerning Montazeri.[61] *Salam* tersely replied in 1995 that, given the atmosphere, it had decided to remain silent on the issue so as not to participate in creating unrest.[62] In this way, the personage and status of the *marja'* became enmeshed in factional rivalries.

The *marja'iyya* issue presented the clerical government with a serious ideological trial which had significant political implications. As Hashim has observed, the "severe crisis of political legitimacy" is "eroding the foundations of the system." The separation of *marja'iyya* and *rahbariyya* "is a major blow to the regime's conception of itself as an Islamic state."[63]

The harsh realities that persisted after seventeen years of rule by the religio-politicians led some Iranians to attribute the government's failures to Islam. This indictment in turn led some clerics "increasingly, though still indirectly, to criticize the religious office of the Guide."[64] Seyyed Mohammad Qomi (son of Ayatollah Seyyed Hasan Tabataba'i Qomi) gave vent to such concerns. By nature, he claimed, state and religion "are incompatible" and thus "must be separated." Since governments inevitably commit violations, it is counter to the interests of Islam that clerics run the state. The experience of the revolution since 1979, he maintained, had only earned Islam and the clergy a bad reputation. Clerics were now identified with "terrorism, torture, bombing, explosions, and hostage-taking," which Qomi said "have no place in Islam." The world perceived Iran's politics as representing Islam, and their example had brought nothing but disgrace to true Islam. Even judging by practical results alone, Qomi maintained, the Islamic government has failed to secure "anything" for the oppressed, who are "even more oppressed now" than before the revolution. In any case, he argued, *marja'iyya* was not an issue for governments to deal with.[65]

ALTERNATIVE THOUGHT

Some leading Iranian intellectuals have begun to stress a similar conclusion. In recent years, Iran has experienced a flowering of "alternative thought" (*andisheh-ye digar*), "the expression of viewpoints that are different from and often in opposition to official policy positions."[66] University professor 'Abdul-Karim Soroush has become their most eloquent spokesman. According to Soroush, the "ideologization of

---

[61] *Resalat*, March 30, 1993.

[62] *Salam*, December 21, 1994.

[63] Ahmed Hashim, *The Crisis of the Iranian State*, Adelphi Paper 296 (London: International Institute for Strategic Studies, 1995), pp. 5, 23.

[64] Lamote, pp. 10-12.

[65] *Kayhan* (London), December 15, 1994, in *DR*, January 20, 1995.

[66] Eric Hooglund, "The Pulse of Iran Today," *Middle East Insight* 11, no. 5 (July-August 1995), p. 41.

religion" is the beginning of its vulgarization and leads to its deterioration. His idea, founded on relativism, stresses that although the sacred texts are unchangeable, human perception of them depends on many variables, including time, period, and location.[67] Soroush also delves into the difference between religion and ideology.[68] With the transformation of faith from *nehzat* (the awakening movement) to *nehad* (ruling institution), the blood which had initially kept the Islamic movement alive had been converted into opium, he said.[69] Faith is not a mold with a fixed cast (*qalebi jehat-dar*), Soroush argued, and Khomeini's movement "will not bear the appropriate fruits" unless his followers nurture "a new understanding of religion [*din*]."[70] Imposing a specific interpretation upon religion gives it a superficial and official mold and makes it dogmatic (*qeshri*) and one-dimensional (*yek bo'di*). Religion is richer (*farbetar*), more comprehensive (*kameltar*), and more humane (*insanitar*) than ideology. It generates weapons, tools, ideals, but is not itself the tool.[71] Religion is like air (*hava*), essential for every human being but lacking a fixed mold. As one of the essentials of its eternality, religion does not strive for a specific historical society. Ideology, by contrast, is like a garment or mantle (*jame va qaba*) designed to fit a particular individual or a medicine prescribed for a specific patient. In sum, religion is like a scale (*tarazu*), lamp (*cheragh*), rope (*risman*), and ladder (*nardeban*)—none has a defined destination.[72]

Moreover, Soroush argued, the rule of the clergy is "based on the logic of power, not the logic of liberty." Using religion as an ideology "makes it intolerant and authoritarian," he said. Government and economics are the province of intellect and reason, not religion. Clerics should be "freed" from state or public financial support so that they are not forced to propagate official views. Religion is for "the lovers of faith," not for "the dealers of the faith."[73]

The relevance of Soroush's ideas to the realities of the Islamic regime is clear. They have led both supporters and critics to compare his role in

---

[67] Eric Rouleau, "The Islamic Republic of Iran: Paradoxes and Contradictions in a Changing Society," *Middle East Insight* 11, no. 5 (July-August 1995), pp. 55-56.

[68] 'Abdul-Karim Soroush, *Farbe-tar az Ideoloji* (Tehran: Sarat, 1993). For an insightful discussion of his thoughts in the context of current politics, see Judith Miller, *God Has Ninety-Nine Names: Reporting from a Militant Middle East* (New York: Simon and Schuster, 1996), pp. 429-64. For criticism of his views, see Jahangir Saleh Pur, "Naqdi bar nazariye 'Farbetar az ideoloji,'" *Jahan-e Islam* 5 (Tirmah 1994), pp. 15-17, 23-27. For Soroush's response to his critics, see 'Abdul-Karim Soroush, "Ideolojik Dini va Din-e Ideoloji," *Jahan-e Islam* 5 (Tirmah 1994), pp. 18-22.

[69] Soroush, *Farbe-tar az Ideoloji*, pp. 114-17.

[70] 'Abdul-Karim Soroush, "Dark dar 'Azizane-ye Din," *Kiyan* 4, no. 19 (Khordad 1994), pp. 2-9.

[71] Soroush, *Farbe-tar az Ideoloji*, pp. 122-23.

[72] Ibid., pp. 125-30.

[73] *LAT*, December 30, 1995; *Kiyan* 4, no. 23 (February-March 1995), pp. 2-36.

reforming Islam to that of Martin Luther in reforming Christianity.[74] His views include an "implicit attack on the institution of the *velayat-e faqih.*" Paradoxically, his challenge was well received by some (primarily younger *mullahs*) who believed that by becoming too closely identified with the state, Islam was in danger of "losing its soul."[75] Many Iranians seem to agree that the clerics' political involvement was "compromising their historic spiritual role" and that it would be better for both Iran and Islam if the clergy "returned to the mosques and left the task of government to professional politicians."[76]

By seeking *marja'iyya* status, Khamene'i wished to eventually attain the powers exercised by Khomeini. His succession inspired him "to be a genuine holy man."[77] He takes "seriously his role as heir to Khomeini's mantle." Though he had failed to gain full theological endorsement, his recognition as one of the *maraje'* (in addition to his political power) undergirds his authority and serves as an important asset. Still, it would be difficult to regard his rulings "as authoritative, binding, superior to those of other eminent jurists . . . and as the guidelines by which the state, society and individuals should conduct themselves." His religious rulings lack jurisprudential authority.[78]

In the long run, theologians (both current and yet to emerge) are likely to constitute a challenge. History has shown that Shi'i theologians are more prone than Sunni *'ulama'* (clerics) to adopt independent political positions. In fact, as one scholar noted, in the case of Khamene'i "the higher clergy attempted to hold the government at arm's length, first by selecting an ancient candidate (i.e., Araki) who would reign but not rule, and then by selecting so many candidates that none could rule."[79] This is an "urgent national issue" as well as a theological question.[80] Yet in the immediate aftermath of Khomeini's death, it seemed "impractical, if not impossible," to combine spiritual and temporal leadership in one person, and "equally impractical" to separate the two roles.[81]

In sum, the *marja'iyya* saga reflects a significant retreat from the most important feat of the revolution, with state interests gaining supremacy over dogma, and religio-politicians over theologians. This constitutes a severe blow to ideology, may prove harmful for Islamism in power, and has already damaged the functioning of the Iranian government. The political-ideological rivalries within the ruling elite further add to the challenges.

---

[74] *LAT,* January 27, December 30, 1995.

[75] Rouleau, "Paradoxes and Contradictions," pp. 55-56.

[76] Hooglund, "The Pulse of Iran Today," pp. 41-42.

[77] Mottahedeh, p. 112.

[78] Bakhash, "The Crisis of Legitimacy," pp. 104, 109, 113-14.

[79] Mottahedeh, p. 115.

[80] Abdulaziz Sachedina, "Who Will Lead the Shi'a? Is the Crisis of Religious Leadership in Shi'ism Imagined or Real?" *Middle East Insight* 11, no. 3 (March-April 1995), p. 25.

[81] Bakhash, "The Crisis of Legitimacy," p. 99.

III

The Struggle for Power:
Pragmatists, Radicals, and Conservatives

By their very nature, revolutionary movements have often deviated from their radical doctrine once they made the transition from opposition to power. Islamic Iran was no exception. As the leader of an opposition movement, Khomeini had depicted a "new Iran" modeled on purely Islamic design. Once in power, however, he (and even more so his disciples) realized that they could not rule by means of slogans alone. Governing required management rather than theorizing about affairs of state. A measure of pragmatism and realism was inevitable.

Once the religio-politicians were firmly in command, a fierce struggle for power became evident within their ranks. Differences emerged for a variety of reasons, including the inherent tension between the doctrine of the revolution and national interests, different interpretations of Islamic law, divergent doctrinal convictions, different political considerations, personal rivalries, and a pure struggle for power. The result was a policy that combined a cautious and pragmatic attitude on some key issues (e.g., economics, relations with some of its neighbors and most European states) and enhanced radicalism toward others (e.g., cultural Islamization, relations with Islamist movements). This struggle to determine the path of the revolution continues.

Western opinion by and large viewed these differences as existing essentially among three distinct factions: pragmatists, radicals, and conservatives. In fact, the situation is more complex, and identifying individuals as members of a specific group is no easy matter. The various trends never actually organized into clear-cut factions—let alone competing parties with coherent, collective ideologies; there were significant subgroups in each, and all proclaimed loyalty to Khomeini's "line." Moreover, it is impossible to distinguish between genuine ideological differences and personal rivalries. Participants frequently change their positions and occasionally even their political alignments—often speaking in pragmatic terms on one occasion, only to voice more radical views on others. As one newspaper noted caustically, it is also true that Iranian officials often speak "sweet words in English to foreigners, but it's strictly Satan-as-usual when they speak Farsi on the home front."[1]

---

[1] *Echo of Iran*, no. 41 (June 1991), p. 17.

Yet considering their entire visions, cumulative statements, and policy priorities, it seems inevitable that they would be classified either as radicals, (relative) pragmatists, or conservatives. Though generalizations are rife with pitfalls of inaccuracy and error, it can be said that those who hold executive power and share the burden of running the state are generally members of the pragmatist faction. Conversely, those outside the administration comprise the bulk of the radicals.[2] But it should be remembered that the former also started out as radicals, fully aligned with Khomeini's doctrines. It was the practical problems of running the government and perpetuating Islamic rule that gave their thinking a belated pragmatic tinge. As the problems facing the regime multiplied, the tendency toward pragmatism became more marked. The regime gradually became more mindful that perpetuating its rule required a measure of realism. Yet the pragmatists never fully retreated from their original vision, nor did the radicals abandon their struggle to attain their goals.

The fact that Khamene'i periodically exhorted the different "camps," "trends," or "wings" (as they were variously described) to maintain their unity demonstrates the intensity of the domestic rivalries. The basic disagreements between the groups were often asserted by their leaders. Rafsanjani, for example, who is often seen as the head of the pragmatists, said that there were "two currents" in Iran, "a radical one and a more moderate one."[3] Hojjat ul-Islam 'Ali Akbar Mohtashami, commonly viewed as leading the radicals, alluded to the depth of such divisions. Khomeini's death, he said, had plunged Iranian society into a period of deep despondency in which the true revolutionaries (i.e., the radicals) no longer "ha[d] a voice" and had been "eliminated from the scene." He accused "some members of a particular faction [i.e., the pragmatists] of spreading venom and distorting facts to prevent us [radicals] from continuing our rightful course."[4] Rivalries were evident from the start of the revolution,[5] but became much more bitter after Khomeini's death.

RADICAL IDEOLOGY AND PRAGMATIC POLICIES

In general, the seventeen years of post-revolution rule indicate an increasing trend toward pragmatism, interspersed with occasional outbursts of radicalism, a pattern that has persisted despite changes in personalities, issues, and alignments.

---

[2] There are, of course, some exceptions. Mohtashami, for example, remained extremely radical even while serving as minister of the interior, and many of those who do not share administrative responsibilities are pragmatists.

[3] *Der Spiegel,* March 25. The Rafsanjani interview is also quoted in *Ettela'at,* March 27, and in *DR,* March 26, 1991.

[4] *Salam,* March 17, in *DR,* April 8, 1991.

[5] For some earlier examples, see David Menashri, *A Decade of War and Revolution* (New York: Holmes and Meier, 1990), pp. 115-16, 147-50, 174-75, 219-25, 268-71, 345-47, 378-84.

In 1979, a confrontation between Prime Minister Mehdi Bazargan (who wished to pursue pragmatic policies) and his radical rivals led to the seizure of the American embassy and an interval of radicalism. In 1981, in response to President Abul-Hasan Bani Sadr's more liberal approach, his opponents forced his expulsion and introduced another period of radicalism. In 1983-84, the religio-politicians introduced an interlude of greater pragmatism that reached its peak in the arms deals with the United States in 1985-86. After that, a new interval of radicalism took hold (as demonstrated by the conflict with the U.S. Navy in the Gulf, riots during the 1987 Hajj, and the election of a more radical Majlis in 1988).

The summer of 1988 introduced a new trend of pragmatism, which found its most profound expression in the approval of the July 1988 ceasefire in the Iran-Iraq War, the reconstruction policy (autumn 1988), and a measure of liberalism associated with the celebration of the first decade of the revolution in February 1989. That was followed by another phase of radicalism, manifested in the disqualification of Montazeri as Khomeini's heir apparent and the latter's *fatwa* against author Salman Rushdie in March 1989. After that, the pragmatists reinforced their power, and the tendency toward pragmatism became more evident, though their attempts to pursue such policies were often blocked (or delayed) by the conservatives.

At the outset of each radical wave, its leaders seized on an issue with which all supporters of the revolution could identify, in order to challenge their rivals. Thus, the 1979 seizure of American hostages targeted Bazargan, the 1981 expulsion of Westernized liberals from power was used against Bani Sadr, the 1986 Iran-Contra affair threatened Rafsanjani, and the 1989 Rushdie *fatwa* targeted Montazeri (and probably also Rafsanjani). All were manifestations of ongoing ideological, political, and personal struggles for power. Unlike the struggle against Bazargan, Bani Sadr, and Montazeri, however, attempts to significantly curtail Rafsanjani's power have thus far failed.

The growth of the radicals' power, which typified the political *milieu* on the eve of Khomeini's death, was reversed with Rafsanjani's election as president in 1989. His first step was to exclude radical ministers Mohtashami (interior) and Mohammad Reyshahri (intelligence) from his government.[6] On the eve of the 1990 election for the Council of Experts (which was empowered to, among other things, select a new Supreme Leader), the struggle reached a new peak. The government then made the Council of Guardians hold examinations for candidates whose proficiency in jurisprudence was not highly regarded.

---

[6] Mohtashami and Reyshahri were replaced by 'Abdollah Nuri and 'Ali Fallahiyan, who were considered radicals at the time (but seemed to have less political clout), were believed to be personally close to Rafsanjani, and presented a less significant challenge than their predecessors. See details in Menashri, *MECS* 1989, pp. 356-59. Nuri gradually distanced himself from the more radical tone and in recent years has expressed more pragmatic views. By contrast, Fallahiyan remained radical and seems to be closer to Khamene'i.

The issue was attended by acrimonious mutual accusations, primarily in the Majlis, where a fistfight broke out between members of the opposing camps. Although the Guardians claimed that decisions on candidates' eligibility were made purely on legal religious bases, the examinations were ultimately used to obstruct the radicals. In fact, among those rejected were leading radicals such as Speaker Mehdi Karubi, Ayatollah Sadeq Khalkhali, and Mohtashami. That they were found to lack sufficient religious credentials to sit on the Council was a humiliating indictment for the *hojjat ul-Islams*, to say nothing of the speaker of the Islamic Majlis. Former head of the Revolutionary Court Khalkhali accused "some elements" of attempting to monopolize the revolution.[7] Having eliminated (to use Mohtashami's word) the radicals first from the executive in 1989 and then from the Council of Experts in 1990, Rafsanjani and his men went on to break the radicals' influence in their main powerbase, the Majlis.

THE 1992 MAJLIS ELECTIONS

The 1992 Majlis campaign has become known as the "mother of all election campaigns" (*umm al-ma'arek al-intikhabiyya*).[8] Although the two competing clerical associations (the JRM and RMT) were restricted to the capital only—due to Khomeini's 1984 prohibition against clerics of one constituency interfering in the electoral affairs of others[9]—each had its supporters in every street and bazaar throughout the country.[10] The election thus typified the larger pragmatist-radical contest.

The JRM was headed by former interior minister Ayatollah Mohammad Reza Mahdavi-Kani, and most of the pragmatists centered around it. They included first Vice President Hasan Habibi, Vice President 'Ata'ollah Mohajerani, Finance Minister Mohsen Nurbakhsh, Foreign Minister 'Ali Akbar Velayati, and former Deputy Foreign Minister Mohammad Javad Larijani. They drew their support from the modern middle class, including government employees, technocrats, professionals, and elements of the business community.[11]

---

[7] *Resalat*, October 1, in *DR*, October 18, 1990. Majlis member Eliyas Harazi characterized the decision as a conspiracy "by one specific faction" to exterminate the others; see IRNA, October 2, in *DR*, October 3, 1990.

[8] *Al-Majallah*, March 18, 1992.

[9] *Kayhan* (Tehran), April 9, 1984; see also *MECS* 1983-4, pp. 433-34. For more on their competition in 1988, see *MECS* 1988, pp. 491-92.

[10] Speech by Khomeini's son Ahmad, quoted in *Abrar*, April 26, and *Salam*, April 27, 1992. He went on to add that the differences between the two were not that wide and that on most basic issues they were in agreement.

[11] Ali Banuazizi, "Iran's Revolutionary Impasse: Political Factionalism and Societal Resistance," *Middle East Report* 24, no. 191 (November-December 1994), p. 4. See also Banuazizi, "Faltering Legitimacy: The Ruling Clerics and Civil Society in Contemporary Iran," *International Journal of Politics, Culture, and Society* 4, no. 4 (1995), pp. 563-78.

The prominent figures of the RMT and those identified with it were commonly known as radicals: former Interior Minister Mohtashami, Majlis Speaker Karubi, former Prosecutor-General Mohammad Musavi Kho'iniha, former head of the Revolutionary Court Khalkhali, former Minister of Intelligence Mohammad Mohammadi Reyshahri, and Deputy Majlis Speaker Asadollah Bayat. Other leading figures close to them were Chairman of the Council of Experts and Imam Jom'a of Qom Meshkini, former head of the Supreme Court Ardebili, and Council of Experts member Ayatollah Mohammad Mohammadi-Gilani. Their support came from student associations and younger, more militant clerics.

Although they were not able to block the government's major policies—e.g., the Economic Plan, acceptance of foreign loans, release of Western hostages in Lebanon—in the Majlis, the radicals nevertheless showed their contempt for the government by using the forum to criticize it. They became a significant, well-organized power group and based their arguments on Khomeini's doctrine. Their key positions in the Majlis (Speaker Karubi, Vice Speaker Bayat, defense committee chairman Mohtashami) added to their influence there.

The pragmatists used the government apparatus to suppress their rivals. Acting in their service, the Council of Guardians used its constitutional role in supervising the elections to disqualify leading radicals: some forty members (out of a total of 270) of the outgoing Majlis, most of them radicals, were found unqualified to run,[12] among them Bayat, Khalkhali, Hojjat ul-Islam Hosein Musavi Tabrizi, Ebrahim Asgharzade, Ghafari, 'Ateqe Sadiqi Raja'i, and former minister Behzad Nabavi.[13] According to the election committee, the reasons for their disqualification were not made public in order to avoid infringement of privacy.[14]

The radicals had hoped that, in the general interest of the revolution and in line with the practices of Khomeini (who had often supported the rights of minority groups as long as they worked within the Islamic consensus), Khamene'i would support them. He, however, stressed the pragmatists' main propaganda line, advising voters to elect representatives who would enact laws that would "enable the duly-elected Government . . . to carry out its work."[15]

And, as is the case in all elections, the incumbent government had a considerable advantage over its rivals. In December 1991, Rafsanjani and his supporters replaced many of the provincial governors. They used government-controlled radio and television (which at the time were run by Rafsanjani's brother, Mohammad) to spread their propaganda, and their contacts with provincial *jom'a imams* (leaders of the Friday prayer) to do so

---

[12] *Salam* (March 31, 1992) wrote that in general, those disqualified all belonged to the same political trend.

[13] *Salam*, April 3, 1992.

[14] IRNA, April 7, in *DR*, April 9, 1992.

[15] Radio Tehran, March 27, in *DR*, March 30, 1992; *Ettala'at*, March 28, 1992.

in mosques around the country.[16] They also used their control over the judiciary to launch investigations of prominent radicals, and then spread rumors concerning alleged offenses. According to the *Echo of Iran*, the pragmatists "shrewdly succeeded in compiling evidence of embezzlement" against individuals such as Ardebili, Ghafari, Hasan Karubi, Asadollah Bayat, and Khalkhali, and released some of it to the public "to destroy their image." Charges for mishandling the Martyrs' Foundation fund (headed by Karubi) were also published. In addition, some government critics (such as Majlis member Qorban-'Ali Salehabadi) were summoned to Evin prison and warned to keep quiet.[17] Others (including Mohtashami and Morteza Alviri) were summoned to the special court for the clergy.[18] An atmosphere "poisoned with rumors" blemished the radicals' reputation.[19] Khalkhali said that the government's actions would "breed dictatorship."[20] The JRM was accused of being "monopolists" (*enhesar-talab*) who wished to liquidate (*hazf*) loyal elements[21] of the revolution in order to "create a one-track Majlis."[22] Despite such vehement protests, the radicals lost this round.

In the 1993 presidential elections, the radicals failed to even nominate a candidate to compete against Rafsanjani. Following the elections, however, the RMT announced the reopening of its central office in Tehran and other locations, a move likely prompted by the size of the vote against Rafsanjani and an assessment that the deteriorating economic situation could be their "ticket to success."[23] Yet while they continued to criticize the government's deviation from the path of the revolution and take it to task for its failures, the RMT's collective activities declined significantly, because members did not "consider the conditions favorable" for such activities.[24] Admitting that their movement was "not involved in political activities in the true sense of the word,"[25] the radicals pledged to continue following Khomeini's path. The pragmatists thus tightened their control over the government, but were limited in their ability to advance their ideology.

---

[16] According to *Salam*, January 14, 1992, the JRM sent "secret bulletins" to the *jom'a imams* which included accusations "against individuals and social and political groups."

[17] *Echo of Iran*, no. 40 (May 1991), pp. 12, 14, 19.

[18] For such practices, see *Salam*, September 21, 1991.

[19] *Salam*, April 21, 1992.

[20] Tehran TV, June 2, in *Echo of Iran*, no. 41 (June 1991), p. 12.

[21] *Salam*, April 30, 1992.

[22] See their complaint to Khamene'i in *Salam*, March 29, 1992.

[23] *IT*, November 5, 1993.

[24] *Salam*, October 21, in *DR*, November 1, 1993.

[25] Mohtashami, explaining their failure to put forward a candidate in the 1993 presidential elections, in *Salam*, May 16 and 17, 1993; see also *DR*, May 28, 1993. They also failed to pose any significant challenge in the 1996 elections.

FACTIONAL DIVISIONS

The two factions represent contradicting attitudes on almost every issue: how strictly to adhere to the dogma of the revolution and what the government's policy and priorities should be. Some experts view the differences between the two factions as revolving mainly around domestic policy,[26] arguing that Iran's foreign policy is generally seen through "the prism of domestic issues"[27] and that "foreign policy is now dependent" on "internal crises."[28] Others claim that "perhaps in no other realm . . . is the impact of factionalism and ideology as apparent" as in foreign policy.[29] Yet the two realms can hardly be separated,[30] and in fact the differences between the two factions encompassed all spheres of life.

The pragmatists demanded that revolutionary slogans be toned down in favor of a policy of expediency. They saw economic rehabilitation as Iran's major task and advocated improving foreign ties, including those with Western and "reactionary" Muslim states. Their policies reflected Rafsanjani's preferred—yet often flexible—ideology.

Rafsanjani declared in 1988 that the days of early Islam had long passed and that "today . . . we live under new conditions."[31] In March 1991, he reiterated the need to adjust ideology to reality.[32] It was no longer necessary, he said later that year, "to speak fanatically" or "chant impractical slogans." Instead, what Iran required was "a prudent [*tadbir*] policy" that could be employed without being accused of "engaging in terrorism [and] without anyone being able to call us fanatics."[33] Iran could safeguard the principles of the revolution "only under the aegis of a rational [*ma'qul*] and logical [*manteqi*] policy,"[34] he said, adding that "[w]e do not consider revolution as being beyond the framework of reasonable methods." We "must not be radical" nor abandon principles and values.

---

[26] Patrick Clawson, *Business as Usual? Western Policy Options Toward Iran* (Washington, DC: American Jewish Congress, 1995), pp. 10, 15. But he, too, is aware that "the positions that each side takes on domestic issues also have foreign policy implications"; see pp. 10-11.

[27] Patrick Clawson, "Alternative Foreign Policy Views among the Iranian Policy Elite," in *Iran's Strategic Intentions and Capabilities*, ed. Patrick Clawson (Washington, DC: National Defense University, 1994), pp. 29, 31.

[28] Laurent Lamote [pseudonym], "Domestic Politics and Strategic Intentions," in *Iran's Strategic Intentions*, pp. 5, 17.

[29] Banuazizi, "Iran's Revolutionary Impasse," pp. 4-5.

[30] Farhad Kazemi, "All Politics is Local," in *Iran's Strategic Intentions*, pp. 49-54.

[31] Radio Tehran, September 25, in *SWB*, September 27, 1988.

[32] Interview in *Der Spiegel*, March 25, 1991. Also quoted in *Ettela'at*, March 27, and *DR*, March 26, 1991.

[33] Radio Tehran, December 20, in *DR*, December 23, 1991. It should be noted that these phrases were deleted from the otherwise lengthy reports of his Friday sermon in *Kayhan*, *Ettela'at*, and *Abrar*. See also *MECS* 1991, p. 385.

[34] Radio Tehran, August 23, in *DR*, August 24, 1992.

"We are not dogmatic. We do not support absolutism."[35] Nateq Nuri said that the pragmatists believed in moderation in accordance with the Koranic verse, "We made of you an *umma* justly balanced."[36]

The pragmatists did not abandon the goals of the revolution, however; they merely sought pragmatic means to achieve them. Moreover, pragmatism prevailed only to a certain degree and in specific areas, and was pragmatic only by Iranian standards. In fact, pragmatism occasionally led to *more* aggressive methods (such as the assertive Iranian approach to the Gulf islands in 1992) or was used as a means of pursuing radical aims.

Moreover, when radical and/or anti-American sentiments ran high, Rafsanjani himself adopted the more extreme rhetoric of Khamene'i and other officials. In May 1989, for example, after Khomeini's *fatwa* against Rushdie, he called upon Palestinians to retaliate against Israel by attacking Westerners and their interests worldwide: "If, in retaliation for every Palestinian martyred in Palestine, they kill . . . five Americans or Britons or Frenchmen," he said, the Israelis "would not continue their wrongs." His choice of targets was based on the "pragmatic" observation that "it is a bit difficult to [kill] Israelis," but "it is not hard to kill Americans or Frenchmen" because there are so many of them "around the world." He also advised the Palestinians to hijack planes, blow up factories in Western countries, and threaten American interests "throughout the world."[37] On the 1994 anniversary of the seizure of the U.S. embassy in Tehran—when anti-American sentiments often run high—Rafsanjani pointed out that when the Americans were still "savages and eating fruit from the trees in the jungle," Iran had a great civilization and thus could not be forced to "surrender" to U.S. demands now.[38] Despite having said all this, however, Rafsanjani was certainly more pragmatic than some of his domestic rivals.

The radicals, for their part, believed Iran could solve its problems by strictly adhering to dogma regardless of changing realities, and criticized government officials for their political impotence[39] and for failing to comprehend the strength of the revolution. Epitomizing this position, Mohtashami excoriated the government for abandoning the "pure stances of the revolution" and failing to "gauge the extent of the honor and prestige of the Iranian system." He accused those who devised Iran's foreign policy of being "overwhelmed with intense fear."[40] The radicals disputed what they perceived as the government's bid to improve ties with the West and especially the United States,[41] and advocated greater efforts

---

[35] Interview with Beirut TV, November 28, in *DR*, December 3, 1993.

[36] *Al-Safir*, November 29, 1993.

[37] IRNA, May 5, in *DR*, May 5, 1989.

[38] Radio Tehran, November 4, in *DR*, November 7, 1994.

[39] *Jahan-e Islam*, May 24, in *DR*, June 4, 1993; *Iran News*, February 9, in *DR*, February 17, 1995.

[40] *Jahan-e Islam*, May 24, in *DR*, June 4, 1993.

[41] To assert that the restoration of ties with the United States would solve Iran's problems

to expand the influence of the revolution beyond Iran's borders. They emphasized that—unlike the government—they remained faithful to the revolution[42] and that weakening them would be in America's interest, for their strength was the only thing preventing the United States from reasserting its hegemony over Iran.[43]

Yet their main criticisms revolved around the government's social and economic policy. The two camps differed in their perceptions of both the priority that economic rehabilitation should have and the policies to achieve it. In the aftermath of the Iran-Iraq War, Rafsanjani (with the general support of Khamene'i) stressed the centrality of economic reconstruction and made it the centerpiece of his 1989 presidential campaign and government program.[44] By contrast, the radicals viewed assigning the highest priority to the economy as a pretext for pragmatism and establishing ties with the West. In 1989, Mohtashami listed Iran's main challenges "[i]n order of priority" as "political, cultural, social and, finally, economic problems." He added that only Iran's enemies stress the primacy of economy (as the pragmatists often did), in order to divert attention from the crucial issues of "political and cultural independence."[45] A year later, he said that the pragmatists' "proposition that we should first address ourselves to economic issues . . . is a mere fallacy. That is simply a pretext . . . to remove the core of the revolution."[46] In 1993, he reiterated: "If you set the economy as the principle and sacrifice everything at its altar, there would remain nothing by which you could be powerful, free, and independent."[47]

The radicals therefore opposed many of the government's initiatives to foster the economy and blocked (or delayed) its reconstruction programs (only to later criticize its failures). When they did stress economic goals, their emphasis was on the need to improve the lives of the underprivileged and advance Iran's economic independence. Toward that end, they called on the government to take control of foreign trade, limit land holdings, impose higher taxes on the rich, and otherwise reform Iran's economic structure and resource management. They criticized the government efforts to facilitate the return of expatriate professionals and encourage investment by exiled capitalists, and railed against private enterprise, debt rescheduling, and negotiating foreign loans. The economic programs that the World Bank and IMF recommended, *Salam* wrote, were designed to

---

was tantamount to considering America "to be God on earth," Mohtashami charged; see *Jahan-e Islam*, October 19, in *DR*, November 10, 1993.

[42] See a typical argument of this type in *Salam*, March 14, 1992.

[43] *Al-Sharq al-Awsat*, March 23, 1992.

[44] Radio Tehran, October 7, in *SWB*, October 10, 1988. For the two camps' different goals and priorities in economic policy, see Menashri, *A Decade of War and Revolution*, pp. 392-93.

[45] *Ettela'at*, December 12, 1989. Similarly, see his interview in *Kayhan* (Tehran), December 11, 1989.

[46] IRNA, November 13, in *SWB*, November 15, 1990.

[47] Clawson, *Business as Usual?*, p. 12 (based on *Salam* and *Akhbar Ruz*, May 17, 1993).

achieve their own "evil imperialist" goals.[48] These "international economic institutions . . . operate within the framework of the West's hegemonic policies," it later added. "We will not be able to satisfy our hunger with the loaf of bread that the West will loan us."[49]

To the radicals, ideology, economics, and foreign relations were interrelated, and thus so was their criticism of their rivals. The radicals criticized Rafsanjani's government for being indifferent to people's suffering, adding that his ministers—mostly technocrats rather than ideologues[50]—had never suffered "poverty and hunger."[51] Such accusations were meant not only to censure government failures but also to stress its abandonment of a primary pledge of the revolution: to improve the situation of the *mostaz'afin.* The radicals accused the government instead of putting itself in the service of the arrogant (*mostakbarin*)—both domestically (the wealthy) and abroad (the superpowers).

For their part, the pragmatists dismissed the radicals as only outwardly (*zahera*) concerned about the weak and accused them of raising such arguments cynically to gain popular support. Whereas the government persistently endeavors to solve problems, the pragmatists said, the radicals "poke sticks through its spokes" and raise "hollow slogans." Rafsanjani called on them to substitute intelligence (*sho'ur*) for slogans (*sho'ar*).[52] The radicals were further accused of providing ammunition to Iran's enemies with their accusations.[53] Vice President Hasan Habibi characterized them as "professional revolutionaries," expert only in raising untimely slogans. Vice President 'Ata'ollah Mohajerani called them "dubious elements" who gamble with popular despair "with pure opportunism, to present themselves [as] . . . an alternative to the present leadership."[54]

The third faction, the conservatives, was much more influential than it appeared. It derived its strength from the conservative clergy, *bazaar* circles, and the traditional middle class; was strongly represented in the Council of Guardians; and emerged as the dominant faction in the fourth Majlis. Its members appeared pragmatic on some issues (such as the

---

[48] *Salam,* January 5, 1993; *Echo of Iran,* no. 60 (January 1993), p. 4.

[49] *Salam,* October 13, in *DR,* October 25, 1993.

[50] One-third of his twenty-two ministers approved in 1989 had studied in the West, eight had Ph.D. or M.D. degrees, nine were engineers, and only four were *hojjat ul-Islam*; see Menashri, *MECS* 1989, pp. 356-59; Radio Tehran, August 19, in *SWB,* August 21, 1989; *Ettela'at,* August 30, 1989. Fifteen of the twenty-three nominees for the 1993 government held doctorates or engineering degrees, including seven who had studied or had practical experience in the United States. By contrast only two clerics remained in the cabinet— Minister of Intelligence 'Ali Fallahiyan and Minister of Justice Isma'il Shushtari; see Menashri, *MECS* 1993, p. 325; *Ettela'at,* August 8 and 18, 1993; IRNA, August 16, in *DR,* August 16, 1993.

[51] *Bayan,* January-February, in *DR,* February 27, 1992.

[52] *Kayhan* (London), April 16, 1992.

[53] See, for example, Rafsanjani's Friday sermon in *JI,* April 18, 1992.

[54] *Al-Majallah,* November 13, 1991.

economy) but radical on others (such as culture). Thus, they advocated the strict application of Islamic law and social and cultural norms, the sanctity of private property, greater freedom for private enterprise, and an economic policy more open to the outside world.[55] Characterizations of them as "economically liberal but culturally hard-line conservatives" and "the embodiment of the unity of the market and of the *chador*"[56] captures these seemingly contradictory attitudes.

Conservatives were less vocal than the radicals but more influential in the institutions of the revolution. Thus, despite the pragmatists' electoral victory, the fourth Majlis was not more supportive of Rafsanjani's reforms. "Ironically," one scholar maintained, the conservatives were an even "greater block to reform" than the radical-dominated Third Majlis. Mindful of the impact of price rises on public transport, the Majlis refused in early 1994 to eliminate the enormous petrol subsidy.[57] They also supported the campaign to counter the Western "cultural onslaught." In recent years, members of this group strengthened their hold over some key positions. Nateq Nuri (who later expressed more radical views himself) replaced radical Majlis Speaker Karubi, Mohammad Yazdi replaced Ardebili as head of the judiciary, 'Ali Mohammd Besharati became interior minister, 'Ali Larijani replaced Rafsanjani's brother as director of radio and television—in addition to conservatives who had held major posts before, such as Mostaz'afin Foundation director Mohsen Rafiqdust.[58] Though many hardliners were driven from office, "they were replaced by social conservatives who had little use for [pragmatist] reforms." Given the narrow base of the regime, says Bakhash, it had to "appear radical on international issues and Islamically correct on social issues."[59] Hardliners thus set the terms of the debate. "They take a 'show me' attitude toward change, shifting the burden of proof to any party proposing change."[60] With decisions defaulting to the radical line, this created a bias in favor of continued extremism: pragmatism has to be defended, while generalized revolution-inspired activity does not. The government is "tied to a hard line" from which any departure "must be justified."[61]

This divisiveness was much deeper than the authorities admitted, but less than often depicted in the West. Nevertheless, in response to a question in 1994 about the major threats facing the regime, deputy Majlis

---

[55] Shaul Bakhash, "Iranian Politics Since the Gulf War," in *The Politics of Change in the Middle East*, ed. Robert Satloff (Boulder, CO: Westview Press, 1993), pp. 71-72; Banuazizi, "Iran's Revolutionary Impasse," p. 4; Ahmed Hashim, *The Crisis of the Iranian State*, Adelphi Paper 296 (London: International Institute for Strategic Studies, 1995), pp. 8-9.

[56] Hashim, pp. 8-9; *NYT,* January 31, 1993.

[57] Hashim, p. 20.

[58] Banuazizi, "Iran's Revolutionary Impasse," p. 5.

[59] *LAT,* February 7, 1994.

[60] Shahram Chubin, *Iran's National Security Policy: Capabilities, Intentions, and Impact* (Washington, DC: Carnegie Endowment, 1994), pp. 68, 71.

[61] Ibid.

speaker Hasan Ruhani said that the primary threat was domestic. "If we maintain our unity at home," he said, "I don't think that any foreign enemy can create problems for us."[62] Rafsanjani managed to keep the domestic rivalry under control and maintain pragmatism, but he failed to use his power to ease the burden of the people or even advance his policies.

---

[62] *Hamshahri*, September 4, 1994.

IV

Rafsanjani: Challenge of the Presidency and the 1996 Majlis Elections

Whereas the major challenge facing Khamene'i was a lack of religious credentials, Rafsanjani's primary ordeal became effective administration of the state. Here he faced two interrelated tasks: asserting his leadership and solving Iran's mounting domestic problems.

THE LOCUS OF AUTHORITY

In the absence of Khomeini's omnipotent command, factional rivalries and the co-leadership of Rafsanjani and Khamene'i worked to further thwart decisionmaking. Relations between the two fluctuated between cooperation and competition. They have long been close associates, publicly supporting each other and cooperating against the regime's opponents. Yet they have also competed for power and held distinctly different views and priorities. Rafsanjani's generally pragmatic approach was often malleable and occasionally inconsistent. Khamene'i's line was no less confusing. Either out of sincere belief or to underpin his religious credentials, he frequently voiced views close to those of the conservatives and occasionally the radicals on topics such as culture and Islamism; at other times, mindful of the need to solve the country's mounting problems, he supported Rafsanjani's economic policies.

Yet both men are aware of their mutual dependence and responsibility for serving the revolution, the people, Iran, and Islam, and overcoming the challenges posed by their common adversaries. Some have used the metaphor of a tandem bicycle to characterize their rule: They labor jointly to move forward, and must coordinate, cooperate, consult, or at least inform each other before any "sharp turns" (i.e., critical decisions).[1]

Which of them occupies the driver's seat remains an open question, however. There appears to be an informal division of labor, with Rafsanjani taking the lead on economic and foreign policy and Khamene'i directing "religious" issues and ties to other Islamist movements. But such divisions are not always completely accurate. Khamene'i has a role in formulating foreign relations, just as Rafsanjani has a say in Iran's attitude

---

[1] See, for example, R. K. Ramazani, "Iran's Foreign Policy: Both North and South," *Middle East Journal* 46, no. 3 (summer 1992), p. 394.

toward Islamist movements. Moreover, foreign relations are not devoid of religious aspects—for example, the *fatwa* against Rushdie and relations with Britain (where he lives under government protection), or the pilgrimage to Mecca and ties with Saudi Arabia. The two leaders seem to discuss crucial issues—and probably also less crucial ones—before making decisions.

Publicly, they support each other amicably. Khamene'i often mentioned their common struggle against the shah since the late 1950s, and having shared a room with Rafsanjani in Tehran in the mid-1960s.[2] In 1984, he described his former roommate as the most "talented, wise, and brave" man he had ever known. "I pray to Allah that he will take [years] off of my life and add them to the life of Rafsanjani," he added.[3] On the eve of the 1992 Majlis elections, Khamene'i praised him again. "Which [previous] head of government was comparable to him?" he asked. "Which of them was as trusted by [Khomeini] . . . . [and] has served the revolution as much as he? If the Imam [Khomeini] were with us now, he would strongly support the present government."[4] He described Rafsanjani as "one of the Imam's most prominent associates and a celebrated pillar of the revolution."[5] Following Rafsanjani's re-election in 1993, Khamene'i described him as "cherished [*mahbub*] by all" and "worthy of the job,"[6] later adding that the president has a "shining personality" and is a "strong arm and eloquent tongue of the revolution."[7]

For his part, Rafsanjani portrayed his relations with Khamene'i as the best two people could possibly have. They had struggled together for some forty years, he said, stood alongside each other since the revolution, and were always in full agreement. "I view him as the most appropriate individual to be leader of the state," he said in 1994. "The rumors about rivalry and competition reflect only the jealousy of others."[8] Reviewing their long struggle later that year, he said: "Now as then, when I have no access to him, I feel weak. My faith in him increases as time goes by."[9]

Their praise of one another notwithstanding, a measure of competition has long been evident between the two, beginning when Khamene'i served as president (and secretary-general of the Islamic

---

[2] *JI*, September 26, 1984. See also his statements quoted in Menashri, *Iran: A Decade of War and Revolution* (New York: Holmes and Meier, 1990) pp. 264, 307, 350-52.

[3] *JI*, November 24, 1984.

[4] *Ettela'at*, March 28, 1992; Radio Tehran, March 27, in *DR*, March 30, 1992. Earlier he denounced some of Rafsanjani's rivals as financially, morally, or ideologically corrupt, and accused them of weakening the system by "poking sticks through the government's spokes"; see *Ettela'at*, February 23, 1992; *Echo of Iran*, no. 49 (February 1992), p. 13.

[5] *Salam, Abrar,* and *JI*, May 30, 1992.

[6] *Abrar, JI,* and *Ettela'at,* June 17, 1993.

[7] IRNA, August 3, 1993 ; Radio Tehran, August 3, in *DR*, August 3, 1993; *Ettela'at*, August 4, 1993; *IT*, August 13, 1993.

[8] *Ettela'at*, June 8, 1994.

[9] *JI*, December 29, 1994.

Republic Party) and Rafsanjani was Majlis speaker,[10] and continuing when Khamene'i became Supreme Leader and Rafsanjani president. Their individual ambitions—Khamene'i to play the role of the Imam and Rafsanjani to consolidate the powers of the executive—were bound to create some competition, in which Khamene'i had several advantages. Unlike Rafsanjani, he has no direct administrative responsibilities and is thus not identified with the executive's failures. Moreover, whereas his is a lifetime position, Rafsanjani's second (and, according to the constitution, last) term as president ends in 1997.

After Khomeini's death, Khamene'i left the driver's seat to Rafsanjani, but grew "far more assertive" in articulating policy and controlling key positions. Rafsanjani and his associates apparently overlooked Khamene'i's potential for becoming "a magnet for the vested interests" threatened by their reforms. Whether out of conviction or political calculation, Khamene'i often adopts positions close to the radicals and conservatives, sometimes to the point of undermining Rafsanjani's policy. After the 1993 elections, Khamene'i began to exercise his political prerogatives even more forcefully and to secure important posts for his protégés.[11]

Rafsanjani appears to have lost power since first being elected president in 1989. Although the 63 percent of the vote he received in 1993 would be considered a comfortable margin of victory in Western countries, it was small in regional and Iranian terms. By comparison, he received 94.5 percent of the vote in 1989, and Khamene'i won 95 percent in 1981 and 88 percent in 1985. In fact, Rafsanjani won less support in 1993 than Bani Sadr in 1980 (76 percent)—the lowest previous for an Iranian president. The results were viewed as "a warning" to him, indicating popular disenchantment with the domestic (mainly economic) situation and disappointment with the president himself.[12]

Economic rehabilitation was Rafsanjani's central theme in the 1989 elections. He promised a "decade of reconstruction" that would extricate Iran from its economic difficulties after eight years of war and improve the lives of the *mostaz'afin* (dispossessed). He described his first term (coinciding with the First Economic Plan) as "successful" and "satisfactory," and promised that the second plan would further stabilize the economy.[13] Whereas under the shah and during the Iran-Iraq War the distribution of wealth had been unfair, he said, since the five-year plan "the wealth of the higher strata is gradually decreasing and the wealth of the

---

[10] See, for example, Menashri, *Iran: A Decade of War and Revolution*, pp. 307-9, 350-52, 390.

[11] Ahmed Hashim, *The Crisis of the Iranian State*, Adelphi Paper 296 (London: International Institute for Strategic Studies, 1995), p. 18; Bakhash, "The Crisis of Legitimacy," in *Middle Eastern Lectures* (Tel Aviv: Moshe Dayan Center, 1995), pp. 113-14; and Roy P. Mottahedeh, "The Islamic Movement: The Case of Democratic Inclusion," *Contention* 4, no. 3 (spring 1995), p. 126.

[12] Tehran TV, May 26, in *DR*, May 28, 1993; *TT*, June 14, 1993; and *JI*, June 14, 1993, in *DR*, June 29, 1993.

[13] See, for example, his broadcast on Radio Tehran, June 3, in *DR*, June 4, 1993.

lower strata is increasing."[14] Eager to complement his achievements, he went as far as to implicitly blame Khomeini for failing to improve their living standards. Moreover, Rafsanjani raised expectations by making promises that would be difficult to keep. On the anniversary of the revolution in 1993, he expressed the hope that "all the problems facing the country" would be solved by the 20th anniversary of the revolution in 1999. Following his election in 1993, he reiterated similar promises, declaring that at the end of the Second Economic Plan, Iran would be developed (*abad*), independent (*mostaqel*), advanced (*pishrafte*), and would enjoy much greater welfare (*morafah*).[15]

People expected tangible results, but many of the economic and foreign policy goals set out at the beginning of Rafsanjani's presidency were "either waylaid or unsuccessfully targeted."[16] 'Ali Akbar Rafsanjani, "once nicknamed 'Akbar Shah', an allusion to his king-like powers" was viewed by many as "a lame duck with an uncertain future."[17] In 1996, Majlis member Hojjat ul-Islam 'Ali Movahedi Savoji even advocated that Rafsanjani be declared "incompetent" and his government dismissed.[18]

Rafsanjani was not wholly to blame for Iran's economic woes, but as head of the executive with influence on other branches of government, he could not evade responsibility. He was also the first president without a prime minister to whom he could shift some of the blame—a situation of his own making, as Rafsanjani had conditioned his candidacy for the presidency in 1989 on the elimination of the premiership.[19] Even before the constitutional amendment, *Abrar* wrote that if the premiership were abolished, the president "would apparently be in an answerable position."[20]

Another area in which Rafsanjani was at a disadvantage *vis-à-vis* Khamene'i was control over the armed forces. Little is known about how Iran makes decisions regarding national security. The Supreme National Defense Council (SNDC) is comprised of clerics, senior military officers, Revolutionary Guard officers, selected diplomats, and political advisors. Rafsanjani is reported to be its active chair, and its decisions "rise above internal divisions." It generally "tends to adopt lowest common denominator positions that associate all groups with policy decisions."[21] Officially—and in reality—Khamene'i seems to be taking the lead.

---

[14] Radio Tehran, February 5, in *DR*, February 8, 1993. See also his 1993 New Year's speech on Tehran TV, March 20, in *DR*, March 22, 1993.

[15] *Salam*, June 15. See also *Kayhan* (Tehran), June 17, 1993.

[16] *FT*, August 13-14, 1994.

[17] *LAT*, December 13, 1994.

[18] *Salam*, January 26, 1996.

[19] The position of the prime minister was eliminated in the amended constitution of 1989; see *MECS* 1989, pp. 349-50.

[20] *Abrar*, May 21, in *DR*, May 22, 1989.

[21] Shahram Chubin, *Iran's National Security Policy: Capabilities, Intentions, and Impact* (Washington, DC: Carnegie Endowment, 1994), pp. 68, 70.

Rafsanjani, who had assumed Khomeini's role as chief of the armed forces shortly before the Supreme Leader's death in the spring of 1989, resigned the post in September of that year in favor of Khamene'i, who thus became responsible for appointing senior military commanders. In January 1995, he appointed Habib Baqa'i as the new commander of the air force. Three months later, he promoted former Deputy Minister of Defense Hasan Firuzabadi (a Basij official with no known military rank) to a major general with nine years' seniority—thereby making him superior in rank to long-serving Revolutionary Guard commander Mohsen Reza'i and army Chief of Staff 'Ali Shahbazi.

Khamene'i said that offering "such a high rank to a Basiji . . . signals respect and recognition for that organization."[22] The move prompted speculation, however, that there was a power struggle between Khamene'i and Rafsanjani. It also indicated that the clerics wished to bolster the prestige of the Basij at a time of mounting internal unrest. Senior commanders in the Revolutionary Guard and regular army had reportedly been reluctant to carry out orders to move against civilian demonstrators (e.g., in Qazvin). There were also reports of discontent among officers and resignations by dozens of Revolutionary Guard commanders (along with many of their men) because of disillusionment with government policy.[23]

Khamene'i was also strengthening his hold over extra-governmental bodies such as the Bonyad-e Mostaz'afan va Janbazan (Foundation of the Dispossessed and Self-Sacrificers) and Bonyad-e Shahid (Foundation of the Martyrs). As one source observed in regard to these largely independent entities, the Majlis "can issue as much legislation as it wants" and the ministers "can issue whatever decrees they want, but the foundations remain immune; they regard themselves as standing aloof."[24]

Another problem facing Rafsanjani was the constitutional limit of two consecutive presidential terms. Vice President for Parliamentary Affairs Mohajerani hinted that "there may be an amendment" to this provision of the constitution.[25] In such a case, he said, Rafsanjani would be the most qualified person for the office. But many resented the idea for constitutional, political, or personal reasons. *Jomhuri-ye Islami* said the amendment would be tantamount to instituting "permanent sovereignty" and thus contrary to the interest of the revolution.[26] *Gozaresh-e Hafte* described "the spirit" of such a change as "disagreeable and reproachable, for it lays the foundations for an authoritarian and autocratic government." Unlike North Korea, Syria, and Libya, the paper added, Iran

---

[22] *Jane's Intelligence Review–Pointer*, June 1995, p. 3.

[23] Ibid.

[24] *Il Sole-24 Ore* (Milan), July 20, in *DR*, July 28, 1995.

[25] *Iran News*, October 30, in *DR*, November 4, 1994. Alternatively, Mohajerani said, Rafsanjani could return to his previous post as speaker; see *Al-Majallah*, November 6, 1994; *Resalat*, November 28, 1995.

[26] *JI*, November 15, 1994.

does not have "a lifetime president."[27] Nateq Nuri rejected the amendment as wrong in principal because it was aimed primarily to favor a particular person. It would signal that the revolution depends on a few individuals, he said, when in fact there are a number of qualified candidates, including himself.[28] Needless to say, Rafsanjani's adversaries—whether out of strict adherence to the constitution or partisan political convictions—rejected the idea out of hand.

While his supporters did not abandon their attempts to extend Rafsanjani's presidency, the president himself neither endorsed nor precluded the possibility.[29] In the seventeen years since the revolution, he has proven to be a shrewd, sophisticated, and successful politician. Despite declining support for the government, Rafsanjani remains personally popular. After eight years as speaker and two terms as president, he has survived the vicissitudes of political changes and remains in the upper echelon of Iranian politics. A pragmatist by Iranian standards, Rafsanjani seems to have correctly diagnosed Iran's troubles and identified the proper remedy. Many Iranians believe that his pragmatic approach is ultimately the only way to extricate Iran from its economic crisis. Yet it is also in this regard that he has failed. Though he has undeniably faced severe challenges, he has thus far failed not only to meet popular expectations but also to demonstrate the necessary determination, persistence, and leadership to pursue his own preferred policies.

Thus, when Mohajerani and Raja'i Khorasani called for some sort of improved ties with the United States, for example, Rafsanjani backed off, showing neither the fortitude to support the proposal nor the courage to denounce it. And when in August 1995 the free market experiment faced criticism, he replaced Vice President and Director of the Planning and Budget Organization Mas'ud Rowghani-Zanjani, one of the architects of his economic program.[30]

Referring to his hardline statements to domestic audiences, the *Echo of Iran* observed that Rafsanjani's "kinder, gentler foreign policy" is not simply "a hoax," but rather that he and his aides know their preferred policies "rile the radicals" and "feel they must feed some 'red meat' to keep them at bay."[31] In general, Rafsanjani proved more successful at convincing Khomeini to take bold steps (e.g., to accept a ceasefire in the Iran-Iraq War) than in exercising leadership as president. In fact, he has often allowed himself to be carried away by waves of extremism.

---

[27] *LAT*, December 13, 1994.

[28] *Salam*, January 28, 1995. *Jahan-e Islam*, November 24, 1994 (in *DR*, December 7, 1994) warned that such an amendment could lead to further deviation in the future from the spirit and principles of the constitution.

[29] In February 1995, he said he would leave the presidency after eight years; see *Abrar*, February 26, 1995.

[30] AFP, August 12, in *DR*, August 15, 1995.

[31] *Echo of Iran*, no. 41 (June 1991), p. 17.

Since first being elected in 1989, Rafsanjani has wasted a lot of time and political capital. Although the ceasefire with Iraq and the death of Khomeini created the kind of "breaks in historic continuity" that often facilitate the acceptance of new ideas,[32] he failed to produce a significant policy change when the time was ripe. Despite these missed opportunities, he still possesses one significant advantage—there seems to be no better alternatives to the policies he advocates for economic rehabilitation.

THE 1996 MAJLIS ELECTIONS

Rafsanjani's more assertive attitude on the eve of the 1996 Majlis elections signaled a recognition that time is running out and that immediate and decisive steps are essential to promote his policies and preserve his stature. The importance of the elections lay at least in part in the Majlis' place in Iran's parliamentary heritage and tradition of revolution. With Khomeini's support it had consolidated its role as a prestigious and powerful institution. In addition to playing a vital role in shaping policy and using its authority to approve ministerial appointments,[33] Khomeini transferred to the Majlis the formal decision on significant issues (e.g., the release of the American hostages, the impeachment of Bani Sadr, and the acceptance of the ceasefire with Iraq). Similarly, the members' speeches in the Majlis are often used to raise controversial issues and criticize the government.

Beyond the elections' immediate importance, the contending factions viewed them as a critical precursor to the 1997 presidential election and a significant round in deciding the outcome of the larger power struggle. Rafsanjani and his supporters sought control of the Majlis to advance their more pragmatic policies; his conservative rivals wished to preserve their strength, use it to advance a genuinely revolutionary stance, and promote their candidate for the presidency.

Salam dismissed Rafsanjani's earlier promise to allow elections free of government interference as a "drug for a dead patient."[34] His instructions, it maintained, were either late or merely "smoke in the eyes." The Ministry of Interior had already appointed key provincial officials (e.g., mayors, district governors, governors-general) to secure their victory—a step taken (according to *Salam*) under pressure from the "right wing" to eliminate the "left." Former Prosecutor-General Hojjat ul-Islam Kho'iniha censured the "ruling masters" of Tehran as vociferous politicians who strive to expand

---

[32] J. Talmon, *Political Messianism: The Romantic Phase* (New York: Praeger, 1960), pp. 24-26.

[33] In 1980, the Majlis even managed to force on Bani Sadr its preferred candidate for premiership, Mohammad 'Ali Raja'i. In fact, Rafsanjani was the first president to receive Majlis approval for all of his candidates.

[34] *Salam*, September 28, 1995.

their power through fraud and mischief.[35] Mohtashami was confident that
in "a free competition, the radical revolutionaries will win."[36] As things
developed, however, the contest was not between the groups that had
competed in 1992, the JRM and RMT, but between factions—the social
conservatives and pragmatist-technocrats—that had both supported
Rafsanjani in 1992.

In January 1996, sixteen of the president's close aides and advisers
formed a list to compete in the elections. In a public statement, they called
for support for the hero of reconstruction, Rafsanjani, as the way to
advance the goals of the revolution and secure Iran's progress.[37] The
group, formally known as the Khedmatgozaran-e Sazandegi-ye Iran
(Servants of Iran's Reconstruction), was led by four vice presidents plus
Central Bank Governor Nurbakhsh and popular Tehran Mayor Gholam-
Hosein Karbaschi, and was thus often referred to as the G-6 or "modern
right." They placed economic construction at the top of their agenda,
stressed the need for administrative expertise, called for support for the
public sector, and seemed to advocate other general policy changes. Their
slogans combined *'ezzat-e Islami* (Islamic glory), *tadavom-e sazandegi*
(enduring reconstruction), and an *Iran abad* (developed Iran).[38] They were
supported by such papers as *Hamshahri*, *Bahman*, and *Iran*.

The conservatives criticized the Khedmatgozaran as an illegal intrusion
by the executive in the legislature's affairs.[39] Not surprisingly, the group
itself saw no such legal problem.[40] Raja'i Khorasani welcomed the move as
a means of creating a healthy atmosphere of competition.[41] The radical
Salam newspaper accused the JRM of rejecting any alternative line,
including that of the Khedmatgozaran.[42] Khamene'i did not yield to
pressures to denounce the group, but advised against any moves likely to
lead to tension and divisions.[43] He approved their decision, but prohibited

---

[35] Ibid., January 21, 1996.

[36] *Famiglia Cristiana* (Milan), October 15, in *DR*, October 16, 1995.

[37] Among the signatories were Vice Presidents Mohajerani and Reza Amirollahi, Minister of
Justice Isma'il Shushtari, Minister of Education Mohammad 'Ali Najafi, Minister of
Economy Morteza Mohammad Khan, Minister of Construction Gholareza Foruzesh,
Minister of Agriculture 'Isa Kalantari, Minister of Transportation Akbar Turkan, Minister of
Communication Mohammad Gharazi, Minister of Cooperatives Gholamreza Shafe'i, and
Rafsanjani's brother Mohammad Hashemi; see *Ettela'at* and *Salam*, January 18, 1996; *Resalat*,
January 20, 1996.

[38] *Abrar*, February 19, 1996.

[39] Majlis member Maryam Behruzi, for example, the head of a socio-religious organization
called Jame'-ye Zaynab, described the move as divisive and accused the Khedmatgozaran of
caring only to safeguard their own position in the next government; see *Resalat*, January 22,
1996. For similar denunciations by Islamic associations and Majlis members, see *Resalat*,
January 22-24, 29, 1996.

[40] See remarks by Mohammad 'Ali Najafi in *Resalat* and *Salam*, January 22, 1996.

[41] *Kayhan* (Tehran), January 24, 1996.

[42] *Salam*, January 24, 1996.

[43] *Resalat*, January 29, 1996.

any ministers from taking part. Rafsanjani stated that although he remained a member of JRM, he would observe neutrality and refrain from supporting any candidate or group.[44]

Both camps perceived the contest as a struggle to determine the fate of the revolution, the destiny of the state, and their own role therein, and they competed fiercely for popular support. The leading figure in the JRM, which had the majority of seats in the outgoing Majlis, was Nateq Nuri. Other prominent figures included Mohammad Javad Larijani and Morteza Nabavi. They adopted some of the old social justice jargon and directed their concern toward Islamic conduct,[45] and were often referred to as the "traditional right." *Resalat* was their main organ.

Ironically, the JRM attacked the Khedmatgozaran with some of the same themes and rhetoric that the RMT had used against the JRM in 1992. Their campaign focused on calls favoring values over reconstruction and revolution-inspired zeal over technical expertise. Thus, Nateq Nuri reminded Rafsanjani that building bridges and paving highways had nothing to do with "preserving revolutionary values." If that were the yardstick by which Islamic governments were measured, he said, Malaysia would be a better model.[46] Their election slogans pledged to "follow the line of the Imam [Khomeini], obey the leadership [Khamene'i], and support Hashemi [Rafsanjani]."[47] They called on the public to vote only for those "who do not weaken the pillars of Islamic thought under the pretext of liberalism and freedom," describing the Khedmatgozaran as liberals seeking Western-style development and soft Islamic principles and accusing them of being willing to establish ties with the United States. "Not only do the new liberals not resist the hegemony of America, . . . they even think about negotiations and relations with the Great Satan."[48]

A few other lists competed alongside these two main groups. The E'telaf-e Grouha-ye Khatt-e Imam (Coalition of Groups Aligned with the Imam's Line), which supported candidates who are "brave, faithful, and follow the line of the Imam,"[49] included some of the more radical groups. Among these were the Mojahedin-e Inqelab-e Islami (Warriors of the Islamic Revolution)—who were led by Behzad Nabavi and whose views were expressed primarily by *'Asr-e Ma*; the Anjoman-e Mohandesin-e Inqelab-e Islami (Association of the Engineers of the Islamic Revolution); and several associations of university professors, students, and teachers.[50] Additional lists included the Jam'iyyat-e Defa' az Arzeshha-ye Inqelab (Association for the Defense of Revolutionary Values)—which was led by

---

[44] *Abrar,* January 22, 1996.

[45] *Independent,* March 15, 1996.

[46] *JI* and *Kayhan* (Tehran), May 1, 1996.

[47] *Sobh,* February 19; *Resalat,* February 29, 1996.

[48] *Iran,* April 10; see also *SWB,* April 15, 1996.

[49] *Salam,* April 15, 1996.

[50] *Resalat,* February 29, 1996.

Reyshahri and stressed cultural values and social justice[51]—and the Ansar-e Hezbollah, a radical faction close to the Revolutionary Guard and Basij whose most prominent spokesmen were Hosein Allahkaram, Ayatollah Jannati, and Mehdi Nasiri and whose views were reflected in *Kayhan* and *Sobh*. The RMT did not run as an electoral list, but its members and organ *Salam* supported some independent candidates.

No fewer than 2,946 candidates competed in the first round on March 8 for the 270 Majlis seats (including 566 in Tehran for 30 seats), as compared with 2,200 in 1992, 1,600 in 1988, 1,584 in 1984, and about 2,000 in 1980. Throughout the country 139 candidates secured sufficient votes in the first round to win seats (compared to 135 in 1992, 179 in 1988, 123 in 1984, and 97 in 1980). In Tehran only two secured seats in the first round—Nateq Nuri and Rafsanjani's daughter Fa'eze Hashemi (compared to two in 1992 and half of the seats in each of the earlier campaigns).

Ultimately, some 35 percent of the seats went to the JRM, another third to the Khedmatgozaran, and 25 percent to independent candidates and other groups (the Coalition of the Imam's Line won some 54 seats). The other 7 percent went to minorities or constituencies in which the results were nullified.[52] The fact that no group won a majority set the stage for a struggle to win a voting majority. More than that, it added yet another obstacle to making clear decisions. *Salam* welcomed the "defeat" of the "right."[53] Some experts concluded that the elections were a "microcosm of pending changes in relations between the clergy and the state, between elected and non-elected organs within the state, and between moderation and extremism in foreign policy." They added that the elections had "irrevocably changed" Iran's internal "political landscape" and discerned "hints [of] a potential change" in its policy, such as moving away from being "more Palestinian than the Palestinians."[54]

The situation was in fact much more complex. Given the legacy of previous elections, it would be premature to draw definitive conclusions about the results of the 1996 Majlis elections at this stage. From the JRM's inception in 1981, its members (or those allied with it) controlled the Majlis. Prior to the 1988 elections, its more radical members broke away to form the RMT and gained control of the House. In 1992, the JRM—which at the time ran under a slogan of "defense of Hashemi" (*hemayat az Hashemi*)—won a decisive victory. Over time, however, the Majlis has taken

---

[51] Reyshahri defended its creation by saying that political organizations were essential for the revolution and the regime, and did not represent divisiveness or the pursuit of power. He accused those stressing reconstruction over social justice of imitating the West; see *Kayhan* (Tehran), February 19 and March 6, 1996.

[52] The number of clerics in the Majlis has gradually been declining. There are roughly 50 in the fifth Majlis, compared to 128 in the first, 127 in the second, 81 in the third and 36 in the fourth. Over the same period, the number of members with modern higher education has risen significantly; see *JI*, May 27, 1992, and April 21, 1996.

[53] *Salam*, March 13, 1996.

[54] *Christian Science Monitor*, April 16, 1996.

a more conservative course. Those aligned with Rafsanjani in 1992 were essentially the same as those who competed against "his" list in 1996.

This confusing circumstance is partially explained by the fact that many candidates appeared on several electoral lists and were supported by various groups. On the Tehran lists for the first round in 1996, for example, ten candidates appeared on both the JRM and Khedmatgozaran lists; eight of them also appeared on the list formed by Reyshahri. (The latter shared eleven candidates with the JRM and ten with the Khedmatgozaran). Moreover, many of the winners were famous people who received support no matter what list they were on. In fact, the election of so many independents indicated a distaste for factionalism. There are also many new faces in the fifth Majlis (some 156 out of 270).[55] Many of those elected in the provinces were unknown—"unopened melons" as some put it—and it is not clear what line they will take. Finally, Iranian politics has shown that alignments and even ideas are often flexible.

The fact that the elections were held on schedule, and the nature of the groups that competed, attest to the degree to which the clerics had consolidated and stabilized their rule since the first elections in 1980. The campaign was restricted to groups that, despite their differences, all claimed to be "followers of the Imam's line." As in 1992, the Council of Guardians exercised its right to "supervise" the elections by disqualifying some 40 percent of the roughly 5,000 candidates—including about forty members of the outgoing Majlis.[56] This mass disqualification effectively precluded genuine change. Thus, it is impossible to regard the elections as a genuine reflection of popular tendencies. Rather than national elections, *Salam* observed, they were elections only of the "right wing."[57] Given these realities, some even wondered whether there was any need for elections at all—the seats had already been designated.[58]

It is similarly difficult to weigh the success of the Khedmatgozaran. Given that they joined the race at a very late stage, their achievements could be considered a success. They may still be able to attract some independent (and even JRM) members and use their control in the executive to advance their line. But again, Rafsanjani was hesitant to throw his full weight behind the new group, and Khamene'i managed to preserve some balance (by allowing them to run but preventing cabinet ministers from officially aligning with them).

Finally, although Khomeini delegated to the Majlis the authority for major decisions, the Majlis is not the most important authority in shaping

---

[55] *Akhbar*, March 14, in *DR*, March 19, 1996; IRNA, March 11, 1996; *Abrar*, April 22, 1996. Only twelve members served in the Majlis from 1980 until 1992, less than ten until 1996.

[56] In 1992, the Council approved the credentials of only 216 of the 255 sitting members who sought re-election. These disqualifications begged the question of how the screening committee had failed to detect their lack of qualifications when they were first nominated.

[57] *Salam*, December 21, 1995.

[58] Ibid., October 11, 1995.

Iranian policy. Although it played a role in such decisions as dismissing Bani Sadr, releasing the American hostages, and accepting Iraq's offer of a ceasefire, this was only after Khomeini had made up his mind and called on the Majlis to give its formal approval. Moreover, even the radical third Majlis (1988-92) approved Rafsanjani's economic plan, including acceptance of foreign loans. This does not mean that the Majlis is an insignificant institution. In fact, compared with other parliaments in the region, it shows more vitality and a greater degree of independence. Its support for Rafsanjani's policy would have given the president greater liberty to advance his programs; it certainly proved capable of hindering some of them (such as subsidies and the Second Economic Plan). Yet the most important policy decisions are made outside the Majlis, and the main obstacles to change (e.g., in attitudes toward cultural Islamization or relations with the West) are disagreements within the top echelon of the political elite (i.e., Khamene'i and Rafsanjani).

There has been no dramatic change in the domestic scene since the Majlis elections and, less than a year before the presidential elections, the political situation remains unclear. At least in their public statements, Majlis members have so far been less critical of the government than their predecessors. Rafsanjani, who failed to use his more impressive electoral victories in 1989 and 1992 in a decisive manner, has not done so since the spring of 1996. At this stage, Rafsanjani seems weaker—and Khamene'i more assertive and influential—than before.

Similarly, the Khedmatgozaran have not used the election results as the basis for a persistent struggle for power, and in fact seem less active than before the contest. Like Rafsanjani, they have failed to demonstrate the determination, resolve, and persistence needed to achieve their goals. As of this writing, they have not announced a candidate for the presidential elections, while their contenders (Nateq Nuri and Reyshahri) are already preparing for the campaign.

Much time remains until the elections, however. The difficult realities at home, which constitute the main challenge for Rafsanjani and his associates, are also the main justification for the path they champion. In fact, the Majlis elections confirmed once again the centrality of the social and economic problems that remain the major challenges facing the Islamic regime, the new Majlis, and President Rafsanjani.

V

Economic Difficulties
and Political Repercussions

Iran's economy is undoubtedly the Islamic regime's most pressing challenge.[1] The expectations the revolution created have so far failed to materialize. Despite pledges to eliminate poverty (*faqr*) and privation (*mahrumiyyat*) and serve the barefoot (*paberahnegan*),[2] the government has failed to improve the lives of the *mostaz'afin* (dispossessed)—even according to some revolutionaries. Economic policy became enmeshed in a fierce doctrinal and political dispute, and economic decay threatens the political stability and more general vision of Islam in power.

Evidently, Khomeini seized power without having laid down solid economic policies. Islamist economic theory was developed in the decades preceding the revolution by such thinkers as Ayatollah Muhammad Baqir al-Sadr (in Iraq), Ayatollah Mahmud Taleqani, and Bani Sadr.[3] Their writings and many of Khomeini's declarations stress general goals of social justice and economic independence, including self-sufficiency reducing dependence on oil revenues, easing the lives of the *mostaz'afin,* and improving services. But they offered no specific programs to achieve these goals, and thus far none has materialized.

Some of the economic policies subsequently adopted proved highly controversial. The evolving challenges were ideological (i.e., the potential failure of Islamism to remedy economic malaise), political (i.e., popular disenchantment and factional rifts), and personal (a challenge to the leadership and particularly Rafsanjani). Some experts went so far as to

---

[1] This chapter is not intended as an analysis of the Iranian economy, but rather focuses on the effect that economic problems have had on the regime and its policies. For a discussion of the Iranian economy, see Jahangir Amuzegar, *Iran's Economy Under the Islamic Republic* (London: I.B. Taurus, 1993); Anoushirvan Ehteshami, *After Khomeini: The Iranian Second Republic* (London: Routledge, 1995), mainly chapter 5; and Eliyahu Kanovsky, *Iran's Economic Morass: Mismanagement and Decline Under the Islamic Republic* (Washington, DC: Washington Institute for Near East Policy, forthcoming, 1997).

[2] Khamene'i's address to the Majlis on May 28, 1992, in *Salam, Abrar* and *JI*, May 30, 1992.

[3] See, for example, Seyyed Muhammad Baqir al-Sadr, *Iqtisaduna*, 4th ed. (Beirut: Dar al-Fikr, 1973,); Seyyed Mahmud Taleqani, *Islam va Malekiyyat* (Tehran: Entesharat-e Masjed-e Hedayat, 1954); and Abul-Hasan Bani Sadr, *Eqtesad-e Tawhidi* (n.p.: Etehadiye-e Anjomanha-ye Islami dar Urupa, 1978). Interestingly, though many senior officials in Islamist movements are scientists, there is a conspicuous lack of economists. Although the leaders of the revolution discuss issues of political structure, social justice, cultural purity, and the international system at great length in their theories of the Islamic state, the economic system is hardly addressed.

maintain that the Islamic regime's economic policies had accelerated its own delegitimization;[4] it certainly has the potential to do so—as some devout revolutionaries fear—if the problems are not effectively addressed.

THE ROOTS OF ECONOMIC HARDSHIP

In the first decade of the revolution, with Khomeini at the helm and the war with Iraq raging, expectations were limited. After the war, however, they grew considerably, often with government encouragement. To meet them, the Islamic regime had to adopt new policies that often deviated from basic ideological convictions. Striving to both "maintain ideals" and also "meet the needs of the people,"[5] Rafsanjani approved the expansion of the private sector, allowed foreign firms to return to Iran, accepted foreign loans, and took other similar measures. Khamene'i generally supported this policy, saying that reconstruction could not be prolonged "for 100 years," and that consequently Iran needs "financial resources and technology" from foreign sources as well as the involvement of its private sector.[6] Yet seventeen years after the revolution—and seven years after the ceasefire with Iraq—even government officials concede that there is continued economic deterioration and growing popular disenchantment.

Contradictory pressures buffeted Rafsanjani. To address immediate expectations and advance the economy he had to implement reforms (e.g., privatization, improving ties with the West) that sometimes caused hardships for the poor and infuriated the radicals. At the same time, he had to lay the foundation for solid, long-term economic growth (to satisfy conservative *bazaar* circles) while also demonstrating loyalty to Islamic doctrine (to satisfy the radicals). Not surprisingly, this proved a "Herculean task."[7]

The cumulative legacy of the shah, the Islamic regime's own policies, and external developments led to a gradual but serious decline in the Iranian economy during the early years of the revolution. The rapid population growth and accelerated urbanization that began under the shah were exacerbated by the flight of the professional class (and with it domestic capital) and the drop in foreign investment caused by the revolution. The war with Iraq added new difficulties, including costly expenditures, destruction of infrastructure near the front lines, and growing numbers of refugees from war-ravaged areas in Iran and neighboring Afghanistan.

---

[4]   Kaveh Ehsani, " 'Tilt but Don't Spill': Iran's Development and Reconstruction Dilemma," *Middle East Report* 24, no. 191 (November-December 1994), p. 20.

[5]   Radio Tehran, October 9, in *SWB*, October 11, 1988.

[6]   *Ettela'at*, September 17, 1988; Radio Tehran, October 14, in *SWB*, October 17, 1988.

[7]   For a more detailed discussion of such challenges, see Kanovsky, forthcoming.

Iran's primary source of revenue is oil, and the world oil glut and resultant decline in prices made it difficult to finance reconstruction. Production dropped below pre-revolution levels as prices—forecast at around $20 per barrel when the First Economic Plan was drafted in 1989— fell to $16-$17, far below the roughly $40 per barrel at the outset of the revolution. Yet the government, "which kept a tight rein on consumption" during the war, had been overspending since.[8] Imports rose from $8 billion in 1988 to $23 billion in 1992—a total of $72 billion over those four years, of which roughly 40 percent was financed by debt. Iran, which had emerged from the Iran-Iraq War with virtually no foreign debt, began to fall behind schedule on its payments on short-term loans in 1992.[9] Though reports are inconsistent, most sources estimate its total debt at the end of 1993 at approximately $28 billion, with $8-10 billion already overdue.[10] *Salam* estimated Iran's total debt at over $36 billion, whereas Mohtashami cited a figure of around $40 billion.[11] Rafsanjani stated in May 1994 that it was $17 billion, of which $10 billion was scheduled to be repaid at an annual rate of $3 billion, with the goal of solving the problem by 2000.[12] The Central Bank, however, predicted that by 2006 Iran's national debt would amount to $18 billion.[13]

Though Iran was eventually able to cut its annual imports to $13 billion in fiscal 1994, it could not escape the heavy burden and severe consequences of earlier consumption. Mohtashami grumbled that debt repayment was "breaking our backs."[14] *Jahan-e Islam* voiced concerns that "an important part of [Iran's] national income" was being "devoured by debts."[15] Other leaders acknowledged the existence of the problem, but not its dimensions nor possible destabilizing influence. Questioned about the debt problem "bedeviling the country" in May 1993, Rafsanjani stated that the situation was "under control."[16] Iran's creditors, however, exhibited "anxiety that Tehran [had] over-reached itself."[17] Iranian officials admitted in 1993 that "few banks are . . . willing to take Iranian

---

[8] *FT*, February 8, 1993. See also Kanovsky, forthcoming.

[9] Patrick Clawson, *Business as Usual? Western Policy Options Toward Iran* (Washington, DC: American Jewish Congress, 1995), pp. 12, 32-33.

[10] *Salam*, December 2, 1993. See also AFP, December 2, in *DR*, December 3, 1993; Ahmed Hashim, *The Crisis of the Iranian State*, Adelphi Paper 296 (London: International Institute for Strategic Studies, 1995), pp. 13-14.

[11] *Jahan-e Islam*, October 19, in *DR*, November 10, 1993.

[12] Radio Tehran, May 31, in *DR*, June 1, 1994.

[13] Referring to these "vague and sometimes contradictory" figures, *Jahan-e Islam*, May 22, 1994 (in *DR*, June 2, 1994) observed that "a clear picture" of the actual debt "cannot be obtained."

[14] *Jahan-e Islam*, October 19, in *DR*, November 10, 1993.

[15] *Jahan-e Islam*, May 22, in *DR*, June 2, 1994.

[16] *Time*, May 24, 1993.

[17] *FT*, February 8, 1993.

risk" until the delays in repayment are rectified.[18] With a debt service burden equivalent to one-third to one-half of its oil revenues, some foreign sources predicted that Iran was "heading for a payment crisis."[19] In early 1993 Finance Minister Nurbakhsh confirmed "some interruption" in honoring letters of credit, but said he hoped to resolve the problem soon.[20]

The most immediate means of doing so was debt rescheduling. In March 1994 Iran signed credit agreements with Germany and Japan[21] that, along with similar agreements signed subsequently with other creditors,[22] rescheduled a total of some $14 billion in debts.[23] The government's critics, who had consistently opposed foreign borrowing, claimed that rescheduling would only create future burdens. Rescheduling provided the government with some breathing space, however, which was important. Whereas, in the aftermath of the war with Iraq, Iranians had argued about whether to accept foreign loans, they now wondered how to repay them and who would provide them with additional loans.

As with many of the causes of Iran's economic problems, the solutions became mired in the policies of the revolution. Although these were first and foremost economic issues, the Islamic regime's attempts to remedy them involved doctrinal controversies and factional disputes. As one Iranian economist observed, "We have a sick economy because of bad politics."[24] Radicals opposed cooperation with international monetary agencies, privatization, and foreign investment—not to mention normalizing relations with the United States. *Bazaari* circles pressured for market liberalization.[25] The Central Bank,[26] economists[27] and Rafsanjani[28] supported privatization and foreign enterprise, but such plans provoked harsh dogmatic opposition. Mohtashami characterized supporters of privatization as having been "deceived by America."[29] *Jahan-e Islam* argued that "handing over" Iran's economy to foreign firms would not resolve Iran's problems but merely allow foreigners "to pillage" Iran's national wealth.[30] The *Iran Times*, suggesting that efforts to privatize the economy

---

[18] *Echo of Iran*, no. 62 (March 1993), p. 17.

[19] AIPAC, *The Iran Issue at the Halifax Summit: An Update on Sanctions Against Iran* (Washington, DC: AIPAC, 1995), pp. 1-7.

[20] *FT*, February 8, 1993.

[21] Radio Tehran, March 12, in *DR*, March 14, 1994.

[22] *IT*, April 22, 29, 1994.

[23] EIU, *Country Report*–Iran, no. 3 (1995), p. 23.

[24] Jamshid Pajuan (referring specifically to Iran's fiscal policy) in *Time*, March 22, 1993.

[25] See remarks by the deputy minister of industry in *NYT*, January 31, 1993.

[26] *Jahan-e Islam*, November 27, in *DR*, December 13, 1994.

[27] See, for example, the proceedings of a conference held in Tehran, IRNA, May 10, in *DR*, May 12, 1993.

[28] *Ettela'at*, June 8, 1994.

[29] *Jahan-e Islam*, November 1, in *DR*, November 1, 1994.

[30] Ibid., November 27, in *DR*, December 13, 1994.

"had never gotten off the ground," claimed that the decision to re-nationalize two firms that had been privatized in 1995 was evidence that privatization was now in "reverse gear."[31]

In addition to high debt, inflation was one of the most pressing economic problems and led to growing popular displeasure. It was in this realm that common people felt most directly and painfully betrayed. Soaring prices put many commodities beyond their reach, while the black market boomed and speculators prospered. As prices rose, *Kayhan* noted in 1982, the "irritation [*a'sab*] index" was moving upward as well. If this continued, the paper added, "economic malaise" would likely "undermine the political success of the revolution."[32] Mocking the government's appeal for "revolution-inspired patience," Hojjat ul-Islam Ahmad 'Ali Burhani observed that a hungry *mostaz'af* "cannot buy bread with patience."[33]

Official statistics put the inflation rate for fiscal 1993 at 22 percent (exactly the same as in the previous year), but such figures were viewed with skepticism by foreign economists.[34] The "undeniable truth," *Kayhan International* wrote, was that prices were rising "at a crazy rate."[35] As a result, the purchasing power of vulnerable groups—primarily the *mostaz'afin*—had "dropped sharply"[36] and the poor were showing growing signs of irritation. *Abrar* wrote that the price rises "made people lose hope in their future" and "put psychological and nervous pressure on society."[37] When in 1993 Rafsanjani's supporters solicited votes with the slogan "every vote is a bullet fired in the heart of the revolution's enemies," his rivals retorted that each additional percentage point of inflation was a bullet fired into the stomach of the *mostaz'afin*.

Typically, officials portrayed the situation sanguinely. On the anniversary of the revolution in 1993, Rafsanjani said he was "greatly satisfied" with Iran's economic performance and that various indices had reached satisfactory levels.[38] The Islamic Republic had followed the revolutionary path "to perfection," he said the following month, and there were "no dark spots" on its "performance record."[39] Khamene'i was similarly optimistic. Iran had managed "to overcome the obstacles" and advance "in all spheres," he said, and looked forward to an even more "bright and glorious" future.[40] Although Rafsanjani reiterated the view that

---

[31] *IT*, August 25, 1995.

[32] This unsigned editorial, published in five installments, included extremely harsh criticism; see *Kayhan* (Tehran), October 17-20, 24, 1982.

[33] *Ettela'at*, November 1, 1982.

[34] *IT*, April 22, 1994.

[35] *KI*, March 1, in *DR*, March 5, 1993.

[36] Ibid., April 15, in *DR*, April 23, 1993.

[37] *Abrar*, May 1, in JPRS, June 8, 1993.

[38] *Echo of Iran*, no. 61 (February 1993), p. 12.

[39] Radio Tehran, March 19, in *DR*, March 22, 1993.

[40] Ibid., November 2, in *DR*, November 3, 1994.

Iran was "traveling on a satisfactory path in all fields" and that economic indicators appeared positive, he conceded that things could be better. "We want construction, . . . material progress, and economic progress . . . so that we will no longer have any poor, . . . deprived classes will no longer feel deprived, . . . [and the] difference between the rich and the poor will be less every day,"[41] he said. "We have no problems," he later added, but "we ought to live even better."[42]

When government officials did admit difficulties, they usually blamed the West for magnifying them in an attempt to "ignite psychological maneuvers" against Iran.[43] This "propaganda ploy," Khamene'i said, was aimed at "creating despondency and despair."[44] They blamed the United States for lowering oil prices to harm Iran,[45] and Saudi Arabia for overproducing.[46] The government also accused the radicals of hindering efforts to remedy the situation. Rafsanjani continued to rely on time-worn themes, advising businessmen "to be fair" and "mindful" of the economic situation and warning that the regime would deal severely with profiteers.[47] He blamed an unholy alliance of producers, middlemen, and retailers (and a conspiracy on the part of certain profiteers and political elements) —but not the government—for creating "a poisoned climate"[48] and Iran's economic problems. In rhetoric reminiscent of the shah's (mostly unfulfilled) pledges, he promised to solve remaining problems by the end of the Second Economic Plan in 1999.[49] Other officials expressed confidence that people who had risked their lives for the revolution would not abandon it "for the sake of a few shortages or high prices." Such imaginary "threats," they argued, exist only in the minds of Iran's enemies, who "continue wallowing in their foolish concepts," unaware of the strength of the revolution.[50]

At this stage, however, the public would accept nothing less than tangible improvements.[51] A *Kayhan International* headline attested to the expectations: "Mr. President, It is Time for Firm Action."[52] Faced with

---

[41] Tehran TV, March 20, in *DR*, March 22, 1993.

[42] Ibid., December 25, in *DR*, December 28, 1994.

[43] *Kayhan* (Tehran), October 11, in *DR*, October 20, 1993.

[44] Tehran TV, January 9, in *DR*, January 10, 1994.

[45] Nateq Nuri in *IT*, December 17, 1993. See also his similar contention in *IT*, March 25, 1994. Rafsanjani claimed that the United States had "created [the slump in oil prices] to harm" Iran; see IRNA, December 18, in *DR*, December 20, 1993; and *IT*, January 14, 1994.

[46] IRNA, March 14, in *DR*, March 14, 1994.

[47] Radio Tehran, October 7, in *DR*, October 11, 1994.

[48] Ibid., October 26, in *DR*, November 7, 1994; and November 4, in *DR*, November 7, 1994.

[49] *Le Figaro*, September 12, in *DR*, September 13, 1994. See also Radio Tehran, February 5, in *DR*, February 8, 1993.

[50] Nateq Nuri in *Resalat*, August 26, in *DR*, September 13, 1994.

[51] *Kayhan* (Tehran), January 26, 1995.

[52] *KI*, November 25, 1993.

growing popular resentment, the government launched a new initiative in 1994 to fight inflation and profiteering. A committee was formed under the president's supervision to combat high prices and coordinate the distribution of essential goods.[53] The Ministry of Justice once again announced severe measures against profiteers and hoarders, including fines, confiscation, imprisonment, and even execution.[54] But previous such efforts had yielded no meaningful results and people had little expectation that the new measures would prove any more successful. Even the pro-government *Tehran Times* depicted the new economic policy as a "tranquilizer" that was unlikely to cure the illness.[55]

DEMOGRAPHIC TRENDS AND SOCIAL DISPARITIES

Economic pressures were exacerbated by population growth, which hampered government efforts to provide essential public services. The population, estimated at 38 million in 1979, is believed to have risen to roughly 65 million by 1996, although official statistics are inconsistent.[56] Iran's Plan and Budget Organization estimated annual population growth at 3.36 percent for the first decade of the revolution and 2.95 percent from 1987 to 1992.[57] According to a World Bank study, annual population growth exceeded 3 percent during the 1980s and peaked at 3.8 percent between 1976 and 1986.[58] Other studies estimated that some 44 percent of Iran's 1991 population was under fifteen years old[59] and 60 percent under twenty. Thus, roughly half the population was born after the revolution.

The threatening dimension of rapid population growth became evident only after the ceasefire with Iraq (and publication of the 1986 census). Since then, however, Iran's family planning program has made impressive gains. UN experts praise it as one of the world's most successful population control programs for "melding religion and *realpolitik*." [60] The government introduced free contraceptives and legalized sterilization. Fertility has since declined sharply and population growth is "beginning to

---

[53] Tehran TV, October 9, in *DR*, October 14, 1994.

[54] *Kayhan* (Tehran), October 15, 1994.

[55] *TT*, May 26, in *DR*, May 26, 1994.

[56] In 1992, the Interior Ministry estimated annual population growth at 2 percent. In 1993 Vice President Hasan Habibi estimated growth at 2.3 percent; see Tehran TV, June 3, in *DR*, June 4, 1993. Health Minister Marandi cited a similar figure in a conference in September; see *Ettela'at*, September 11, 1993. The government's Statistics Center put it at 3.17 percent; see *Kayhan* (London), July 22, 1993.

[57] *Ettela'at*, July 12, 1993.

[58] Rodolfo A. Bulatao and Gail Richardson, *Fertility and Family Planning in Iran* (Washington, DC: World Bank, 1994), p. 4.

[59] *Le Monde*, April 6, 1993.

[60] *JP*, July 8, 1995. See, similarly, *FT*, September 1, 1994.

moderate." [61] Though this is a significant change with important long-term consequences, in the short term the earlier (and still high) population growth has hampered government economic and social planning.

Meeting growing demand for education is one such challenge. As under the shah, pre-university education expanded rapidly but remained largely theoretical and lacking in quality. Many schools operated on two and sometimes three shifts, with classes containing as many as seventy students. Though facilities for higher education also expanded significantly, capacity continued to lag behind demand and some qualitative deficiencies persisted. The ratio of applicants to admissions remained roughly the same as in the late 1970s (about 10:1), with the number of rejected applicants growing rapidly. In the 1993 academic year, more than one million applicants took exams for some 130,000 university places. [62] There was a large exodus of veteran professors (following the revolution and during the war with Iraq) and shortages of classroom space and basic teaching materials (laboratory equipment and even books).

Housing was no less a problem in the 1990s than in the 1970s. According to official statistics, there was a shortage of 3.7 million housing units in the mid-1980s, causing rents to rise faster than incomes. According to a 1983 survey, families in Tehran were spending as much as 82 percent of their incomes on rent. [63] In the early 1990s, nearly 25 percent of all Iranian families did not own apartments. At best, officials predicted, "the current situation would prevail" for the next two decades. As a result of growing demand and rising inflation, rents spiraled out of control and became yet another major cause of public disillusionment. [64] Similarly, ordinary Iranians had to search frantically for affordable healthcare, often turning to the black market for basic drugs. *Kayhan International* described medical services as "a mess, and the system, if any, . . . at best chaotic." [65] The newspaper advised the government to take the issue "very seriously," lest it create "public resentment and discontent." [66] The situation deteriorated further in mid-1995, after a Health Ministry decision to limit imports of many drugs. [67] Unemployment (particularly among the young), shortages of basic utilities (including drinking water and electricity), the shrinking value of the riyal, and many other problems pressed hard on ordinary people.

[61] Bulatao and Richardson, pp. 2, 13, 20-22, 31-32.

[62] *Kayhan* (London), April 29, in JPRS, May 21, 1993.

[63] *Iran Press Digest* (Economic Bulletin), July 14, 1987. According to 1981 statistics, 1.4 million families in Tehran shared only 900,000 apartments; see *Kayhan* (Tehran), April 25, 1983.

[64] *IT*, December 31, 1993. See also *Kayhan* (London), July 29, in *DR*, August 6, 1993; *Kayhan* (Tehran), June 3, 1995.

[65] *KI*, October 21, 1993.

[66] Ibid.

[67] *JI*, September 4-6 and 9, 1995; *Kayhan* (Tehran), September 10, 1995.

Yet while the poor suffered, the rich continued to lead pleasant lives, and there was a growing sense that the revolution had abandoned the lower strata. In addition, corruption and official misconduct (sometimes involving clerics) gave economic privation a moral dimension.[68] Aware of the cynicism and skepticism that has long governed popular attitudes toward Iranian officials' statements and their personal conduct, Khamene'i urged them to avoid excessive consumption (*asraf*) and ostentatious lifestyles (*tajamolgara'i*). He admonished those who traveled in expensive cars, held lavish marriage ceremonies, and occupied the luxurious houses of the shah's former dignitaries.[69] Yet, according to one Iranian source, the problem was so deeply rooted that it was unlikely to be removed by "superficial affectations" because "some government officials and MPs are the prominent examples" of such conduct.[70] *Kayhan* asked rhetorically why government agents traveled in expensive cars, and how Majlis members could justify their lavish lifestyles.[71] As one citizen complained, "You never see a Revolutionary Guard or a *mullah* having to queue for anything."[72]

These disparities have been highlighted in recent years by a series of corruption and fraud scandals involving government officials. The 1995 Bank Saderat affair broke all records and became known as "the theft of the century." Morteza Rafiqdust (brother of Mohsen Rafiqdust, the head of the Bonyad-e Mostaz'afan—a charitable foundation that had become a huge industrial conglomerate) and seven others were charged with embezzling nearly $450 million from the bank.[73] Ayatollah 'Ali Meshkini, head of the Assembly of Experts, tapped into the popular sentiment that those involved in the scandal had not only harmed the economy but tarnished the dignity of the system. When ordinary people commit a crime, he said, they are "immediately pursued, imprisoned, locked up, and ruined." But "when it is a big shot," the authorities "merely move him from one town to another and give him another post maybe even higher than his previous post."[74] Majlis member Mohammad Baqer Tavakoli described the culprits as "economic terrorists" who should be declared the "corrupt of the earth" (*mofsed fil-arz*) and severely punished.[75] Ultimately, one offender was sentenced to death, two (including Morteza Rafiqdust) to life imprisonment, one acquitted, and the rest given shorter terms.

---

[68] See Chapter VI.

[69] *Ettela'at*, August 15, 1991; *Echo of Iran*, no. 43 (August-September 1991), p. 12.

[70] *Echo of Iran*, no. 43 (August-September 1991), p. 12.

[71] *Kayhan* (Tehran), August 18, 1991. A cartoon in the satirical magazine *Gol Aqa* typified such sentiments: an old car and two people on motorcycles driving into the Majlis as a luxury car drives out; the cartoon is described in *Al-Safir*, June 10, in *DR*, June 25, 1992.

[72] *FT*, March 6, 1990.

[73] See, for example, comments in *Kayhan*, January 10 and 14, and February 5, 1995; *Salam*, January 10 and February 27, 1995; *JI*, February 5, 1995; *Jahan-e Islam*, February 5, 1995.

[74] *Akhbar*, July 22, 1995. See also *Sunday Telegraph*, August 6, 1995; *JP*, August 16, 1995.

[75] *Salam*, February 27, 1995. *Mofsed fil-arz* is a term for those who transgress Islamic law.

In early 1995, cleric and Majlis member Majid Naderi was found guilty of fraud.[76] During the same period, several officials in the Ministry of Transportation, Ministry of Education,[77] customs service, and other government departments were arrested on similar charges.[78] Similar cases involved senior officials at Iran's state tobacco company,[79] the Tehran city council,[80] and the Sepah Bank.[81] Speaker Nateq Nuri asked the authorities to prevent such acts of corruption lest they threaten the revolution.[82] With Iran "already beset by crippling economic problems, the suggestion that the banking scandal is only the tip of an iceberg of endemic corruption is unlikely to improve the flagging fortunes" of the regime.[83]

These are only a few examples of a much larger phenomenon that led many Iranians to feel that, in some respects, the clerics in power were not much different from those they had replaced—a devastating feeling for a people who had supported the Islamic revolution as a means of change. The reports of widespread corruption "prompt comparisons between the rule of the *mullahs* and the last days of the Shah."[84] The "political clergy," added one scholar, "abused its power and amassed great wealth, which contributed to the growing chasm between themselves and the traditional clergy" and "debas[ed] the spiritual value of the clerical establishment" by their "corrupt behavior."[85] Religion, another scholar added, "has become a cover for greed" and corruption. The regime's inherent contradiction—wealthy *mullah*-bureaucrats preaching virtue to the poor—"engendered rampant anger and cynicism,"[86] and gave greater validity to the fears of some clerics that the malpractices of the religio-politicians would be attributed to Islam as a whole.

The government's radical critics painted a dark portrait of the situation and projected even gloomier future prospects. Mohtashami foresaw "extremely dangerous consequences" from the government's economic policies.[87] Rafsanjani had made "lavish promises" of extensive welfare schemes, he said, but "not even one" of them had materialized. Instead, prices "spiraled enormously," foreign exchange rates "started a swift upward trend," the affluent became wealthier, and the gap between rich

---

[76] *Kayhan* (Tehran), February 5, 1995.

[77] *Ettela'at,* July 30, 1995.

[78] *Iran,* February 7, 1995.

[79] *Kayhan* (Tehran), September 18, 1995.

[80] Ibid., August 16, 1995.

[81] *Salam,* March 6, 1995; *Kayhan* (Tehran) and *Ettela'at,* July 22, 1995.

[82] *Kayhan* (Tehran), February 5, 1995.

[83] *Sunday Telegraph,* August 8, 1995.

[84] Ibid.

[85] Hashim, pp. 7, 24.

[86] Edward G. Shirley [pseudonym], "Fundamentalism in Power: Is Iran's Present Algeria's Future?" *Foreign Affairs* 74, no. 3 (May-June 1995), p. 39.

[87] *Salam,* May 16 and 17, 1993. See also, *DR,* May 28, 1993.

and poor widened. Iran's economic policy was tantamount to "letting the economy run amok." If it continued, he warned, "catastrophe will occur."[88]

For their part, the *mostaz'afin* felt that although they had borne the main burden of the revolution and the war with Iraq, only the rich had become richer. Montazeri pointed to the paradox in 1983: "Today, the heavy burden of the revolution, the war, and the resultant shortages is pressing far more on the lower strata" than on the upper strata, who enjoy a large share of the existing services and commodities but contribute precious little at the front lines of the revolution and war.[89] The *mostaz'afin*, he continued, are the "main owners" of the revolution,[90] yet those whose children "avoided going to the front" are its primary beneficiaries.[91] Majlis economic committee spokesman Mohammad Khaza'i said that it was unacceptable to an Islamic regime that "one part of the population walks around with stomachs bloated from malnutrition, while the stomachs of another part are bloated from over-eating."[92] Khomeini himself spoke with distaste of the gulf separating the "shanty-dwellers" (*kukh-neshin*) and the "palace-dwellers" (*kakh-neshin*), and warned that if the mentality of the latter prevailed the revolution would be in real danger.[93]

But the gap has persisted and even widened since his death, and criticism of the clerical regime has intensified. Mohtashami accused the government of serving the rich[94] and complained that soaring inflation had wiped out the value of salary raises for the poor. In this sense, he claimed, the situation in Iran was even worse than in capitalist countries. While the government raises prices to international levels, he said, it does nothing to prevent the people from being "crushed under the burden of debilitating inflation."[95] "Clearly," he said, "there is greater welfare . . . for the rich," but "[a]ll people unanimously agree that life is significantly more difficult today than yesterday" for the poor.[96] Ayatollah Sadeq Khalkhali added that under 'Abbas Amir Hoveyda (the shah's hated prime minister) prices were at least stable, whereas they were now rising by the hour.[97] These derogatory comparisons with the West and the shah's reign were the harshest possible indictments for the Islamic regime.

---

[88] *Jahan-e Islam*, May 27, in *DR*, June 15, 1993. See also *Salam*, July 27, 1994.

[89] *Kayhan* (Tehran), November 24, 1983; see also his speech quoted in *Kayhan* (Tehran), November 7, 1988.

[90] *JI*, November 21, 1984.

[91] *KH*, May 22, 1985; *Kayhan* (Tehran), May 1, 1985.

[92] *Kayhan* (Tehran) January 8, 1983. See also *Kayhan* for similar remarks by Ayatollah Mohammad Mo'men Qomi (April 10), Rafsanjani (February 26 and March 31), and Khamene'i (March 30, 1983).

[93] Radio Tehran, March 21, in *DR*, March 24, 1983.

[94] *Al-Majallah*, March 18, 1992.

[95] *Salam*, July 27, in *DR*, August 11, 1994.

[96] *Salam*, May 5, 1992.

[97] *Kayhan* (London), April 16, 1992.

Kayhan International wondered who was really responsible for the current "state of chaos." Galloping inflation, economic mismanagement, and indifference toward the lower economic strata had made life for ordinary Iranians "intolerable and miserable." Social justice, at one time a major ideal of the revolution, seemed to have become its last priority and, "if current trends are any indication, . . . may never come."[98] People's trust in government policy, it added a month later, was "decreasing daily along with their purchasing power."[99] In 1994, six years after the end of the war with Iraq, it wrote that "at best . . . the situation had deteriorated" and the "bitter reality" of the government's failure was now "clearly visible."[100] It dismissed policies such as displaying price tags on goods as gimmicks that were likely to meet the same fate as hundreds of previous efforts. "Rhetoric has far outstripped reality," it said, adding that in addition to people's purchasing power, their "morale and tolerance" were also in decline.[101]

Every basic textbook of Islamic economics stresses that an Islamic system is free from poverty and hunger, *Salam* wrote, and therefore "given the poverty and suffering of the masses" in Iran, is it "even possible to call [it] an Islamic society?"[102] Judge Burhani had argued in 1982 that a society with such huge social gaps had no right to call itself Islamic.[103] *Jahan-e Islam* (owned and edited by Khamene'i's brother Hadi) was bitterly critical of the government. No serious effort had been made to end spiraling prices, it wrote, and whenever the regime did formulate a policy, it failed completely.[104] Referring to a renowned *hadith* (a saying attributed to the Prophet)—"*Al-mulk yabqa' ma'a al-kufr wala yabqa' ma'a al-zulm*" ("a regime can survive blasphemy but not injustice")—a reader queried *Jahan-e Islam* whether the discrimination, favoritism, price-gouging, nepotism, shortages, and socio-economic gaps were not all clear signs of injustice.[105]

Some critics targeted Rafsanjani directly. Referring to one of his sanguine statements, *Salam* attacked "dreamers" who are happy with the situation and criticize the press for reporting problems[106] or attribute their failures to foreign foes and local capitalists.[107] Mohtashami ridiculed the president for imagining that he could solve the problems through Friday sermons or inciting people against foreign or domestic foes.[108] *Payam-e Daneshju-ye Basiji* said that neither Iran's external nor domestic enemies

---

[98]   *KI*, November 25, 1993.
[99]   Ibid., December 15, 1993.
[100]   Ibid., May 26, in *DR*, June 7, 1994.
[101]   Ibid.
[102]   *Salam*, January 31, 1995.
[103]   *Ettela'at*, November 1, 1982.
[104]   *Jahan-e Islam*, July 5, in *DR*, July 11, 1994.
[105]   *Jahan-e Islam*, January 31, 1995.
[106]   *Salam*, January 28, 1995.
[107]   Ibid., January 30, 1995.
[108]   Ibid., February 8, 1995.

could have possibly contributed even 1 percent to the prevalent hardships, attributing them instead to the government's policies and incompetence and charging Rafsanjani with the responsibility.[109] His officials had made "[a]ll of the decisions that led to the current situation," it said.[110] *Omid* similarly mocked the government's tendency to attribute all failings to the shah or foreign powers and absolve itself of responsibility. "The blows that we have inflicted on our economy are harsher than the conspiracies of the East and the West combined," it wrote. How was it possible to cite national independence as a major gain of the revolution and then claim that "we don't have a say in what is going on in our 'independent' state?"[111] There were calls for the government to resign.[112]

[109] *Payam-e Daneshju-ye Basiji,* January 25, 1995.

[110] Ibid., March 14, 1995.

[111] *Omid,* March 12, 1995.

[112] *Salam,* December 9, 1995.

VI

Popular Opposition, Riots, and the Government's Response

Popular discontent did not find its expression only in Majlis debates, scholarly discussions, and the press. There were numerous strikes, assassination attempts on senior officials (including Rafsanjani and Khamene'i), bombings (frequently resulting in heavy casualties), and occasional riots.[1] Demonstrations, strikes, and acts of violence have been a repeating occurrence since the 1979 revolution; the riots of the 1990s, however, proved extremely worrisome for the regime because the participants were primarily ordinary young people, their grievances touched upon some basic failures of the government, and the target of their attacks embraced some symbols of the regime. Although the connection between riots in various cities is not clear, there was unquestionably a chain reaction. Rafsanjani typically dismissed these as "small incidents" that were "blown way out of proportion." Compared with the 1992 riots in Los Angeles, he said, they were "very small," adding that in Iran, "the people are with the government."[2] But the regime was nonetheless concerned—and for good reason.

GROWING POPULAR UNREST

The riots in Shiraz began on April 15, 1992 as a demonstration by disabled war veterans protesting the mismanagement of funds by the Bonyad-e Mostaz'afan, and turned into a general demonstration against government policies. A month later, citizens in Arak protesting the government's treatment of residents of the city's shanty town clashed with security forces, setting fire to and destroying parts of the city hall, government offices, and other institutions of the revolution. On May 30, similar attempts to prevent illegal housing construction spread the riots to Meshhed, where participants again set fire to a number of vehicles and buildings. Riots, albeit on a lesser scale, were also reported in other cities. Khamene'i blamed the incidents on a foreign "conspiracy" aimed at turning public opinion against the government.[3] Though some citizens

---

[1] This chapter deals primarily with popular uprisings and other manifestations of growing criticism within Iran in the 1990s. It does not discuss external opposition movements.

[2] Rafsanjani interview, *Middle East Insight* 11, no. 5 (July-August 1995), pp. 7-14.

[3] Radio Tehran, June 10, in *SWB*, June 12, 1992; see also *NYT*, June 11, 1992.

may face difficulties and be discontented, he said, "they are not ruffians." Rather, the success of the revolution had made Iran "a very big power" and led its enemies to employ "harassment and mischief."[4] The opposition, however, maintained that these were "only some" expressions of growing popular disillusionment with the clerical regime.[5]

On February 1, 1994, disturbances were reported in Zahedan, where "plotters" smashed windows of residential buildings and damaged vehicles, including those of the security forces. Again, the government blamed foreign elements who aimed "to make the active presence of the people look pale" on the anniversary of the revolution.[6] This was followed by the bombings of Zahedan's City Hall and Jom'a Mosque on March 2, an explosion in midtown Tehran on April 19, an attempt on the life of the *jom'a imam* in Meshhed on April 22, and a blast at Iran's most important mosque, the Imam Reza mausoleum in Meshhed, on June 20. Observers highlighted both the sectarian aspects of these incidents (instigated by rumors that a Sunni mosque had been destroyed in Meshhed) and their link to economic difficulties in the Baluch-Sunni areas.[7]

Riots were triggered in Qazvin on August 3 by the Majlis' rejection of a bill to recognize the region as a province, thereby depriving it of larger government allocations. Officials again claimed that the events were "exploited by opportunists"[8] and blamed "anti-social elements" for initiating them.[9] Rafsanjani said the unrest lacked any political basis and that "all of these events are distorted by the West." He reiterated that the severity of these events was "a long way from the Los Angeles riots."[10]

Signs of popular resentment proliferated in early 1995. On January 14, a sporting event turned into a clash with authorities in Meshhed. Four days later, a clash among soccer fans developed into a political protest. Local press reported "acts of vandalism."[11] Opposition sources stressed the political implications of the youthful rioters' "anti-regime slogans" and clashes with the Revolutionary Guards, claiming that this was yet another expression of public rage. The young generation, a joint statement by some opposition movements said, faces a "rotten life today and feels concern over its uncertain future."[12]

---

[4]   Radio Tehran, June 12, in *SWB*, June 15, 1992.

[5]   Voice of Iranian Kurdistan, June 2, in *DR*, June 3, 1992. Foreign observers also viewed the riots as "a sign of serious disaffection"; see *FT*, June 12, 1992; *NYT*, June 1, 11, and 12, 1992.

[6]   *Kayhan* (Tehran), February 1, 1994; Radio Tehran, February 1, in *DR*, February 3, 1994.

[7]   AFP, February 2, in *DR*, February 2, 1994. On the Sunni challenge, see Laurent Lamote [pseudonym], "Domestic Politics and Strategic Intentions," in *Iran's Strategic Intentions and Capabilities*, ed. Patrick Clawson (Washington, DC: National Defense University, 1994), pp. 15-17.

[8]   IRNA, August 4, in *DR*, August 5, 1994; *Hamshahri*, August 4, in *DR*, August 12, 1994.

[9]   AFP, August 5, in *DR*, August 5, 1994.

[10]   *Le Figaro*, September 12, in *DR*, September 13, 1994.

[11]   *Kayhan* (Tehran), *Jahan-e Islam, Resalat,* January 21, 1995.

[12]   Voice of Iranian Kurdistan (radio), February 5, in *DR*, February 6, 1995.

Economically-motivated riots continued in Islamshahr and Akbarabad (southwest of Tehran) on April 4. It was the first major unrest to reach the outskirts of the capital. The immediate cause was a reduction in the water supply and a rise in public transportation fares. Rioters armed with clubs and stones damaged public buildings and vehicles, gas stations, and banks. They disarmed police officers before Revolutionary Guard anti-riot units intervened and sealed off the area. Slogans of "Down with the Islamic Republic" and "Down with Rafsanjani, Down with Khamene'i" were reportedly raised.[13]

Many people were killed or arrested in the riots and demonstrations, and some of the latter were later executed. The government imposed a news blackout on the riots, but gave extensive coverage to subsequent pro-government demonstrations. It resolved not to give the opposition credit for being able to organize such riots (particularly because it had long claimed to have practically eliminated the opposition), nor to present the riots as "popular" or politically motivated. It therefore stressed their limited nature and the supposed role of foreigners in inciting them. Tehran blamed the disturbances on anti-revolutionaries and hooligans, and accused foreigners of being eager to use their propaganda to highlight such incidents.[14]

Yet the Islamic regime was genuinely concerned by the popular nature of the uprisings and the grievances (e.g., inflation, unemployment, housing) that inspired them.[15] *Jahan-e Islam* warned that when people's legitimate wishes are ignored, an "abscessed tumor" evolves.[16] Typically, it quoted "the man in the street" as wondering why the government "fails to accept the truth" that the patience of the people had been totally exhausted (*tamam shode*).[17] *Sobh* wrote that instead of dismissing the riots as arising from isolated issues (like the water supply), the authorities should examine the wider context of growing popular disenchantment, such as rising inflation and other hardships facing the lower strata.[18] The riots were a warning signal for the government, reflecting popular displeasure with domestic realities. The scale of the disturbances, the predominance of young people among the participants, and the grievances they voiced pointed to the perilous nature of the situation.

Similarly worrisome to the government was the response of the security forces: slow to react and initially ineffective. This, according to some experts, "exacerbated latent tensions between the country's political and

---

[13] *Independent*, April 5, 1995; AFP, April 4 and 5, in *DR*, April 5 and 6, 1995; *Ha'aretz*, April 5, 1995; Voice of Mojahed (radio), April 5, in *DR*, April 6, 1995.

[14] *TT*, April 8, 1995; *Salam*, April 8, 1995; AFP, April 5, in *DR*, April 6, 1995.

[15] *Salam*, April 8 and June 2, in *DR*, June 3, 1992.

[16] *Jahan-e Islam*, August 8, in *DR*, August 12, 1994. See also *Resalat*, August 8, 1994.

[17] *Jahan-e Islam*, January 31, 1995.

[18] *Sobh*, April 10, 1995.

military leadership."[19] Moreover, there were already "rumblings of discontent within the armed forces" due to low salaries and economic hardships[20] that may have led some members to identify with the sentiments motivating the rioters. In Meshhed, the government was eventually forced to mobilize special Basij units from different locations to restore order.[21] It set up special Revolutionary Guard forces known as 'Ashura battalions (rapid-deployment forces specializing in anti-riot tactics) to combat domestic unrest.[22] The commanders of the Revolutionary Guard garrison in Qazvin reportedly refused to use force to put down the riots, and the 'Ashura battalions were airlifted into Qazvin to quell the disturbances, "which they did rather brutally."[23] After that, "the army . . . made its position clear: it will not shoot Iranians in the streets."[24]

With the risk of a spontaneous social explosion "quite real," internal security was reinforced and the Revolutionary Guard was redeployed from positions on the border with Iraq "to concentrate around big cities." In addition, the Basij was reorganized in October 1993 and given the specific assignment of maintaining domestic law and order. In February 1994, the minister of the interior was given wide powers to enforce security within the country.[25] In September 1995, the Revolutionary Guard announced programs to expand the 'Ashura battalions in metropolitan Tehran.[26] Rapid-deployment forces, the government believed, were an important means of suppressing its internal enemies.[27]

Encouraged by the riots, the opposition depicted the Islamic regime as increasingly unstable and expressed renewed optimism that it could be overthrown. The head of the National Resistance Council (NRC), Mas'ud Rajavi, called the "heroic uprising" in Zahedan a manifestation of the illegitimacy of the "crisis-stricken clerical regime" and an "indicator of the extent of public rage and aversion against the regime." Rajavi blamed "the *mullahs*' regime" for having "discredited freedom, democracy, and Islam" and promised to soon "bring [NRC leader] Maryam to Tehran."[28] The

---

[19] Michael Eisenstadt, *Iranian Military Power: Capabilities and Intentions* (Washington, DC: Washington Institute for Near East Policy, 1996), p. 41.

[20] Ahmed Hashim, *The Crisis of the Iranian State*, Adelphi Paper 296 (London: International Institute for Strategic Studies, 1995), p. 28.

[21] Asef Bayat, "Squatters and the State: Back Street Politics in the Islamic Republic," *Middle East Report* 24, no. 191 (November-December 1994), p. 11; *Economist*, June 13, 1992.

[22] *Ha'aretz*, June 10, 1992; Voice of Mojahed, June 10, in *DR*, June 11, 1992; Eisenstadt, p. 41.

[23] Hashim, p. 29; *IHT*, October 8-9, 1994; Bayat, p. 11.

[24] Edward G. Shirley [pseudonym], "Fundamentalism in Power: Is Iran's Present Algeria's Future?" *Foreign Affairs* 74, no. 3 (May-June 1995), p. 37. See, similarly, Bayat, p. 11.

[25] Lamote, p. 10.

[26] *Ettela'at*, September 11, 1995; *JI*, September 12, 1995.

[27] *JI* and *Salam*, September 18, 1995.

[28] Voice of Mojahed, August 5, in *DR*, August 5, 1994. See, similarly, *Famiglia Cristiana* (Rome), August 10, in *DR*, August 4, 1994.

Voice of Iranian Kurdistan said that the 1995 riots reflected the "rebellion of a generation that has been deprived" by Islamic rule. Popular dissatisfaction, it said, had turned into "an active volcano."[29] Some even viewed the riots as the harbinger of a new revolution.[30]

Although the opposition may have overrated the significance of the riots, the government underestimated them. Despite the evidence of growing unrest, the regime cited its popular support and the vigilance of the public as effective tools to quell the opposition's designs.[31] Rafsanjani depicted the government as "stronger and more stable than any other regime in the world,"[32] and attributed this to the people's trust in their leaders. The revolution enjoyed even greater support than in its early days, he maintained, and though certain ignorant people (i.e., his domestic rivals) provided foreigners with "grist for propaganda," most acknowledged the revolution's achievements and continued to support it.[33] The regime had "reached such political maturity," Khamene'i said, that "no power can bully Iran."[34]

Through a combination of indoctrination, institutionalization, and suppression, the government has so far managed to preserve political stability. Its main indoctrination line has been that the regime represents true Islam and that therefore any opposition to it is anti-Islamic. Thus, Khamene'i stressed that those who "dearly love" the Koran and the Prophet have a "commitment to the Islamic Republic."[35] The weakness of the opposition is a significant government asset. The various opposition movements have been divided, sterile, and lacking in organization and determination. Moreover, the different factions have neither offered a viable alternative ideology (such as nationalism) nor included significant members of important groups (i.e., the military or clergy) around which to rally. In fact, the immediate threat of instability has thus far proven less severe than some observers believed at the time. The government has managed to suppress the riots and prevent their growth to threatening proportions. But the very nature of such popular unrest, the grievances voiced, and the participation of ordinary citizens (many of them young) are undoubtedly a major concern for the regime. Moreover, even the government could not deny that the problems facing the people are grave and their willingness to protest their disillusionment more marked than in the past.

---

[29] Voice of Iranian Kurdistan, February 5, in *DR*, February 6, 1995.

[30] *Al-Majallah*, April 16, in *DR*, June 21, 1995.

[31] Radio Tehran, February 2, in *DR*, February 2, 1994.

[32] Ibid., February 3, in *DR*, February 3, 1994.

[33] Ibid., February 11, in *DR*, February 14, 1995.

[34] Ibid., August 31, in *DR*, August 31, 1994.

[35] *Jahan-e Islam*, February 1, 1994.

LIMITS ON FREEDOM OF EXPRESSION

The Islamic Republic "remain[s] an anomaly amid revolutionary regimes, an authoritarian government with some elements of licensed pluralism. . . ."[36] By regional standards, the government allows its domestic critics some freedom of expression, albeit only within narrow limits. The radical press—*Salam, Bayan, Jahan-e Islam*, and *Payame-Daneshju-ye Basiji*, for example—voice harsh criticism of the clerical regime. Some new journals (e.g., *Kiyan, Goftegu*) carry penetrating discussions and critical debates. Clearly, "there are signs of resilience and even vitality" in Iran's vibrant intellectual life.[37] These signs of political openness should not be mistaken for genuine freedom, however.[38] As Human Rights Watch asserts, the "apparent intensity of public debate, variety of publications, and wealth of artistic achievements" create only "an illusion of unrestricted discourse."[39] Freedoms "are allowed only as long as the inviolability of Islamic tenets, the irreversibility of the revolution, and the absolute sovereignty of the *faqih* are not questioned."[40]

Prime Minister Mehdi Bazargan recalled that when, in the early days of the revolution, he complained to Rafsanjani about the lack of freedom, Rafsanjani replied: "When the shah gave us freedom, we drove him out of the country. We shall not repeat his mistake." Indeed, as Bazargan observed shortly before his death in 1995, the regime relentlessly eliminates all viable alternatives. "They have not allowed the people to breathe," he said. "They have nipped all efforts toward freedom in the bud. The prospects for the future are extremely frightening."[41]

Though it is true that "compared with some countries in the region," the Iranian press "presents a range of views," the scope of permissible dissent or criticism is extremely narrow and "limited to partisans of the ruling movement."[42] Newspapers not aligned with the clerical regime have found it increasingly difficult to steer a viable course between reliance on the government's avowed adherence to free expression and compliance with the arbitrary limits it placed on such expression—particularly because

---

[36] Fred Halliday, "An Elusive Normalization: Western Europe and the Iranian Revolution," *MEJ* 48, no. 2 (spring 1994), p. 321. See also Anoushiravan Ehteshami, "After Khomeini: The Structure of Power in the Iranian Second Republic," *Political Studies* 39, no. 1 (March 1991), pp. 148-57.

[37] Ali Banuazizi, "Iran's Revolutionary Impasse: Political Factionalism and Societal Resistance," *Middle East Report* 24, no. 191 (November-December 1994), p. 2.

[38] Shaul Bakhash, "Iranian Politics Since the Gulf War," in *The Politics of Change in the Middle East*, ed. Robert Satloff (Boulder, CO: Westview Press, 1993), pp. 78-79.

[39] Human Rights Watch, *Guardians of Thought: Limits of Freedom of Expression in Iran* (New York: Human Rights Watch, 1993), p. 1.

[40] Jamshid Amuzegar, "Islamic Fundamentalism in Action: The Case of Iran," *Middle East Policy* 4, nos. 1-2 (1995), p. 25.

[41] *Frankfurter Rundschau*, January 12, in *DR*, January 13, 1995.

[42] Human Rights Watch, *Guardians of Thought*, p. 125.

the boundaries between what is permissible and what is forbidden have never been defined and "laws are applied selectively and inconsistently."[43] The government takes harsh steps against those it perceives as having transgressed those boundaries, however. In August 1993, for example, *Salam* editor and vocal government critic 'Abbas 'Abdi[44] was arrested on a warrant issued by the Revolutionary Court.[45] *Salam* publisher Kho'iniha was summoned to a special clerical court to face charges of slander against government officials.[46] A cartoonist who was sued for slander and sentenced to a year in prison for an allegedly derogatory depiction of Khomeini in *Farad* in April 1992 had his sentence increased to ten years on appeal by the government prosecutor.[47]

Repression is not limited to liberal opponents of the regime; articles (in publications such as *Bayan*, *Jahan-e Islam*, and *Payame-Daneshju-ye Basiji*) and speeches by devout revolutionaries who argued that the government was not radical enough were also restricted or prohibited. In a 1993 interview in *Salam*, for example, *Bayan* editor Mohtashami complained that "the atmosphere of our mass media and press" is not "favorable [or] healthy."[48] In January 1994, the authorities prohibited Mohtashami from making a scheduled speech in Sari. His hosts informed him that the governor had demanded that the speech be canceled.[49] In August 1995, he was invited to a conference at Tehran's Teachers Training College, but was not allowed to enter and could only deliver a short speech outside the gates.[50]

To make matters worse, "a large part of the government's mechanisms of control and censorship falls outside the law," with the regime employing various methods to intimidate its critics into silence.[51] Thus, for example, though the government never officially closed *Bayan*, according to Mohtashami the pressure on those "in society [and] in government institutions" who cooperated with the monthly magazine—and the constant "obstructionism" it faced—"all helped to stop the publication."[52]

---

[43] Ibid., p. 2.

[44] AFP, November 27, in *DR*, November 29, 1993.

[45] *Salam*, August 28, 1993. 'Abdi was sentenced to a year in prison with a suspended sentence of forty lashes of the whip. See *Salam*, December 25, in *DR*, December 27; AFP, December 25, in *DR*, December 27, 1993.

[46] *Salam* and AFP, August 28 and 29, in *DR*, August 30, 1993; *IT*, August 20 and September 3, 10, and 17, 1993. *Salam* was shut down for three days prior to the 1996 Majlis elections.

[47] *IT*, October 22, 1993.

[48] *Salam*, May 17, in *DR*, May 28, 1993. The *Salam* interviewer was no less critical, inquiring about the existing "poisonous atmosphere" and whether it was disseminated by certain "power centers."

[49] *Salam*, January 25, 1994. For another accusation by Mohtashami of government suppression of its rivals, see *Iran News*, February 9, in *DR*, February 17, 1995.

[50] *Salam*, August 17, 1995; *Akhbar*, August 19, 1995.

[51] Human Rights Watch, *Guardians of Thought*, pp. 5, 39-49, 111-13, 128.

[52] *Jahan-e Islam*, October 19, in *DR*, November 10, 1993. Outright opponents of the regime

In October 1994, 134 intellectuals wrote an open letter to the government protesting state "censorship and harassment" and demanding that it "restore freedom of thought, expression, and publication."[53] Apparently, it had little effect. A report on freedom of expression in Iran states that government repression "gathered pace" in 1995 as "vigilante violence continued throughout the year, encouraged by state officials and religious spokesmen" and that "intrusive restrictions on everyday life continued."[54] Even Iran's thriving film industry came under fire. More than 200 filmmakers petitioned for an end to government interference in scripts, production, funding and distribution of films; in response the government banned the export of any film conveying a "negative image of Iran."[55]

Many open letters purportedly signed by army officers and former officials have been published, although it is difficult to establish their authenticity. Most conspicuous was an open letter by General 'Azizollah Amir Rahimi, former commander of Tehran's military police, in which he condemned summary executions ordered by Revolutionary Court, demanded political reforms, and called on the government to "step down and organize free elections." He warned the clerics that their rule would lead to the "total annihilation of Iran and Islam," pointing out that nothing in Islam condoned what the clerics were doing and urging the formation of a "national salvation government."[56] In a subsequent interview, he complained that Iranians were "hungry and tired" and lacked freedom. "I wish to lead a military coup to change the existing conditions in Iran," he said, "but regrettably I do not possess sufficient military power to do that."[57]

A few days before his death in January 1995, Bazargan criticized the regime for the arrest and torture of several writers and editors. In his view, "not even 5 percent" of the Iranian population supported the regime. The scope of corruption was astonishing, freedom of expression was thwarted, and the smallest protest gathering was forcefully suppressed. Followers of his Freedom Movement were harassed and their publications and gatherings banned.[58] Although the government did not give it much attention, Bazargan's death was nevertheless an occasion to commemorate

---

did not enjoy even that much freedom.

[53] AFP, October 25, in *DR*, October 28, 1994; *Kayhan* (London), October 27, November 3, in *DR*, November 21 and 23, 1994. The *Tehran Times* dismissed most of the signatories as ex-communists who, under communist rule, would not have been allowed to even express support for freedom; see *TT*, October 30, in *DR*, November 8, 1994.

[54] Human Rights Watch, *World Report 1996* (New York: 1995), pp. 276-79.

[55] Human Rights Watch, *Guardians of Thought*, pp. 94-102; *LAT*, December 30, 1995.

[56] *Independent*, September 28, in *DR*, September 28, 1994; AFP, November 1, in *DR*, November 1, 1994. Rahimi had taken part in Mosaddeq's nationalist movement in the early 1950s, spent years in the shah's prisons, and regained his rank following the revolution.

[57] *Al-Majallah*, November 6, in *DR*, November 18, 1994.

[58] *Frankfurter Rundschau*, January 12, in *DR*, January 13, 1995.

his doctrine and path.[59] Renowned Tehran University philosopher 'Abdul-Karim Soroush described Bazargan as "a sincere, faithful, combative, and scholarly Muslim." Soroush came close to explicitly denouncing the clerics in power, saying that "contrary to the politicians and sellers of religion, [Bazargan] never made a business out of religion"—he was a *bazargan* (merchant) by name but not by character.[60]

The ruling elite deemed Soroush's views as blasphemous. Ayatollah Ahmad Jannati called for the elimination of such "harmful freedoms."[61] Nateq Nuri added that those who, like Soroush, view religion as a mere body of moral and ethical guidelines, also believe that society should be administered by so-called scientific management. "Should we obey irreligious people and delegate the governing of society to them?" he asked rhetorically.[62] A group of clerics criticized those who under the guise of intellectualism were making inroads on theocratic government.[63] *Kayhan* vehemently attacked the tendency among some intellectuals to issue "all sorts of ridiculous statements" that serve as grist for propaganda by foreign enemies. It equated such statements with the bombing of a mosque by the opposition during the Iran-Iraq War.[64]

In July 1995, Soroush was physically assaulted by pro-government students after being invited to lecture at Isfahan University. In response to the growing climate of political repression, some 107 academics wrote to Rafsanjani urging him to take steps necessary to insure that constitutional rights were observed.[65] *Kayhan* supported the students' behavior, and wondered why a university would invite a speaker who expresses a philosophy hostile to basic tenets of the revolution.[66] In August 1995 a Tehran publishing house, Morgh-e Amin, was set on fire by armed Hezbollahis who threatened the publisher's life, beat, and detained him, claiming that a book he had published, *God Only Laughs on Mondays*, contained sexual scenes and attacked Islamic values and the war against Iraq.[67]

Ayatollah Jannati, *Jomhuri-ye Islami*, and *Kayhan* (among others) supported the attack, claiming it was the implementation of Khomeini's will. Mohajerani, by contrast, lamented that an entire bookstore had been

---

[59] *Ettela'at*, January 27, 1995; *JI*, January 28, 1995.

[60] 'Abdul-Karim Soroush's speech at the ceremonies honoring Bazargan, January 26, 1995 at Hoseiniye Ershad; see Soroush, "He Who Was Bazargan by Name and Not by Attribute," *Kiyan* 4, no. 23 (February-March 1995), pp. 2-36; in *DR*, July 21, 1995. See also *LAT*, June 6, 1995. For more on Soroush's views, see Chapter II.

[61] Radio Tehran, August 25, in *DR*, August 29, 1995.

[62] *Resalat*, August 29, in *DR*, September 13, 1995.

[63] IRNA, September 17, in *DR*, September 20, 1995.

[64] *Kayhan* (Tehran), May 31, 1995.

[65] *Iran*, July 25, 1995.

[66] Ibid. and *Kayhan* (Tehran), July 25, 1995.

[67] See *Salam, Akhbar*, and *Kayhan* (Tehran), August 24, 1995; AFP, August 24, in *DR*, August 25, 1995.

set on fire in order to show disapproval of one book which had already been removed from the shelves.[68] *Salam,* claiming that this only added to the book's popularity, questioned how Jannati—a theologian member of the Council of Guardians—could defend criminals who set bookstores on fire.[69] *Salam* was in turn criticized for supporting corrupt authors.[70]

In October 1995, Soroush was attacked again, this time at Tehran University, by students shouting "Death to fascism" and "Death to anti-*velayat-e faqih.*"[71] The university's Islamic Society condemned the attack, arguing that universities are a place for clashes of opinion and that the elevation of thought is contingent upon freedom of speech.[72] Two days later, pro-Soroush students at Tehran University organized a demonstration to protest the fascist behavior of the Ansar-e Hezbollah (Supporters of Hezbollah)—the first implicitly anti-government protest of such scale on campus since 1981. Unrest spread to other universities, including Shahid Beheshti and the technological university of Isfahan.

Foreign Minister 'Ali Akbar Velayati claimed that "the Soroush issue" had affected Iran's international standing. Soroush's statements, Velayati said, had inflicted a serious blow on Iran's independence and its national cohesion, and had weakened the regime. He compared Soroush's views with those of Ahmad Kasravi, a nationalist author who was assassinated by Islamic activists in 1946.[73] Khamene'i later equated Soroush's views with sedition and warned that the Islamic system "will slap [those who express them] in the face."[74] In the wake of growing criticism of Soroush and the threats against him by the Ansar-e Hezbollah, his wife expressed concern for the lives of herself and their children.[75]

Salam observed that the ruling elite do not allow anyone to claim better qualifications to run the government than they. Those who do risk sharing the fate of Rushdie and Kasravi—awaiting an assassin.[76]

---

[68] *Ettela'at,* August 24, 1995. *Ettela'at* (August 26, 1995) joined in rejecting the action, claiming that it was unacceptable that, seventeen years after the revolution, unidentifiable groups of armed Hezbollahis would take the liberty to carry out such actions.

[69] *Salam,* August 28, 1995.

[70] Ibid., September 3, 1995.

[71] Ibid., October 16, 1995.

[72] Ibid., in *DR,* October 31, 1995.

[73] Ibid., October 26, 1995. In a December 1995 statement, Soroush responded that the picture Velayati had painted of him was that of an impostor or a prophet, and questioned whether someone who lacked access to the mass media and was constantly accused of spying, treachery, and of being Rushdie, Kasravi, and Malkom Khan (a leading intellectual at the turn of the century who supported the Westernization of Iran) could weaken the pillars of the regime. Comparing him to Kasravi, he said, was essentially a threat on his life. See *Salam,* January 2, 1996.

[74] *LAT,* December 30, 1995.

[75] *Salam,* October 30, 1995.

[76] Ibid., January 28, 1995.

VII

Iran's Domestic Challenges and Regional Ambitions

Iran's major domestic developments—the loss of Khomeini's omnipotent leadership, factional struggles for power, and growing economic distress—overshadowed its foreign policy in the 1990s. At the same time, regional trends and events such as the disintegration of the Soviet Union, the 1991 Gulf War, the Arab-Israeli peace process, and the spread of Islamism—combined to redefine Iran's regional stature and environment. These changes offered Iran new opportunities but also presented it with challenges and dilemmas.

IRANIAN FOREIGN POLICY: NATIONALISM VS. ISLAMIC ORDER

On the whole, the Islamic Republic's pursuit of its goals has been based on the ideology of the revolution, a measure of realism, and considerations of both national interests and those of the ruling regime. Although national considerations were alien to Khomeini's general principles and theory of foreign relations (particularly within the Muslim world), his regime nonetheless chose to conduct its regional policy from a perception of Iran's state interests. Thus, despite his supranational ideology (including the assertion that there are no differences between Muslims), Iran's post-revolution constitution stipulates that only a Shi'i of Iranian origin can be president of the Islamic Republic.[1] Similarly, Khomeini insisted that the Gulf be called Persian,[2] and did not preclude close relations with Arab nationalist and atheist Ba'thi Syria.

Khomeini was in fact in an awkward position. One scholar summed up Khomeini's dilemma as follows: as head of state, "he cannot disavow the idea of the nation-state," but as an Islamic leader, "he cannot make his commitment to the national idea too strong or his commitment to the *ummah* too weak."[3] The result was a "dual policy" wherein the logic of "state

---

[1] In fact, in the first presidential election, Khomeini disqualified one of the candidates—Jalal al-Din Farsi—after it was disclosed that Farsi's father was an Afghani.

[2] Khomeini even rejected Ayatollah Khalkhali's proposal to name it the "Muslim Gulf"; see *Kayhan*, May 29, 1979. In May 1981, Prime Minister Mohammad 'Ali Raja'i issued a statement saying that Persian Gulf was the "correct historical and original name," and ordered its use in all official documents; see Radio Tehran, May 7, in *SWB*, May 9, 1981.

[3] James Piscatori, *Islam in the World of Nation-States* (Cambridge, UK: Cambridge University

interests and of the revolution coexist uneasily"[4] in a mixture of national considerations and revolutionary ideology. In contrast to the shah's rule, Islamic Iran thus "makes policy in a more untidy and altogether less consistent manner." Its "decisionmaking is subject to the play of domestic political forces" that "often pull in different directions."[5]

Initially, Khomeini viewed all governments (particularly in Muslim countries) as illegitimate in principle, declared his intention to conduct relations with people over the heads of their leaders, and upheld isolation as a new ideal for Iran's foreign policy. (Only through isolation could Iran become truly independent, he said.)[6] Yet realities forced Iran to conform to a certain extent to some accepted norms in foreign relations. Gradually, Islamic ideology was subordinated to Iran's national interests[7] because "the primary political arena, even for avowed Islamic 'internationalists' who take over governments, soon becomes the existing nation-state."[8] Within five years of the revolution, Khomeini announced that Tehran wanted to establish "relations with all countries" (with the exception of the United States, Israel, and South Africa). Not to do so, he said, would be "against reason and Islamic law."[9] Beliefs were also often subordinated to business; as one diplomat observed, Iran was "consciously and wisely putting the religious aspects of the revolution in second place and trying to promote trade first."[10] The regime became increasingly mindful of both its opportunities and its limitations, and calculated the costs and benefits when formulating policy. Thus, in most cases in which the interests of the state and the ideology of the revolution clashed, the former triumphed.

Yet the vision of the revolution was not completely abandoned. Parallel to its official state-to-state policy, Iran maintained its links with popular Islamist movements such as those in Lebanon, among the Palestinians, and in Central Asia. And Tehran occasionally pursued the ideology of the revolution to the point of impairing its national interests—it has not hesitated, for example, to imperil its relations with foreign countries in its pursuit of anti-revolutionaries in Europe.

Press, 1986), p. 111.

[4] Ahmed Hashim, *The Crisis of the Iranian State*, Adelphi Paper 296 (London: International Institute for Strategic Studies, 1995), p. 45.

[5] Shahram Chubin, *Iran's National Security Policy: Capabilities, Intentions, and Impact* (Washington, DC: Carnegie Endowment, 1994), pp. 65-66.

[6] Khomeini's speech broadcast on Radio Tehran, November 3, in *SWB*, November 5, 1981.

[7] See David Menashri, "Khomeini's Vision: Nationalism or World Order?" in *The Iranian Revolution and the Muslim World*, ed. David Menashri (Boulder, CO: Westview, 1990), pp. 40-57.

[8] Roy P. Mottahedeh, "The Islamic Movement: The Case of Democratic Inclusion," *Contention* 4, no. 3 (spring 1995), p. 108.

[9] *Kayhan* (Tehran), October 29, 1984. For a similar view expressed a year later, see *KH*, November 11, 1985.

[10] *LAT*, January 1, 1995.

After Khomeini, this "two-track foreign policy"[11] became even more puzzling. It coalesced with domestic disputes during a period of fierce factional strife and indecisiveness. The pressing need to respond to profound regional changes seemed to "gradually, but surely, [turn] the doctrines and practices of Iranian foreign policy on their heads."[12] The result, one newspaper wrote, was vague and unclear signals that indicated an attempt "to be all things to all people": revolutionary to the Islamic radicals, yet "moderate and reasonable to European and Asian countries whose trade and investment" Iran sought.[13] It remained unclear which of its often contradictory statements "represent[ed] new policy, [which were] really a smoke screen, and [which] reflect[ed] simple confusion."[14] That outsiders had difficulty discerning Iranian priorities is not surprising, given that Iranians themselves had similar difficulties. *Jahan-e Islam*, for example, wrote that Iran's regional policy had been "plunged into ambiguity and it is impossible to portray a clear picture of it."[15]

Iran's regional policy came under fire from both sides of its political spectrum. Some critics questioned the advisability of strictly pursuing the doctrine of the revolution; others conversely blamed the government for abandoning doctrine. The former argued that the days when Iran could "offer a mixture of sloganeering and realism as an attractive pattern for oppressed movements" had long passed.[16] Revolutionary purists argued that Iran lacked "a correct analysis of the regional situation," and instead advocated greater activism reflective of its "powerful and righteous stance."[17] Mohtashami accused the architects of foreign policy of "political impotence"[18] and dismissed their policy as "unsuccessful."[19] *Jomhuri-ye Islami* claimed that Tehran remained a silent spectator to events in a manner unsuitable for a revolutionary nation.[20] With its self-imposed silence and policies "swathed in ambiguity," the paper queried, "Are there not . . . eyes that see and ears that hear" Khomeini's vision?[21]

---

[11] Ali Banuazizi, "Iran's Revolutionary Impasse: Political Factionalism and Societal Resistance," *Middle East Report* 24, no. 191 (November-December 1994), pp. 4-5.

[12] R. K. Ramazani, "Iran's Foreign Policy: Both North and South," *Middle East Journal* 46, no. 3 (summer 1992), p. 393.

[13] *IT*, October 1, 1993.

[14] Ibid.

[15] *Jahan-e Islam*, June 2, in *DR*, June 16, 1993.

[16] *Hamshahri*, February 9, in *DR*, February 23, 1993.

[17] See, for example, an editorial advocating greater activism entitled "Foreign Policy Needs Reform," in *Jahan-e Islam*, June 2, in *DR*, June 16, 1993.

[18] Ibid., May 24, in *DR*, June 4, 1993.

[19] Ibid., May 20, in *DR*, June 1, 1993. See also Patrick Clawson, "Alternative Foreign Policy Views among the Iranian Policy Elite," in *Iran's Strategic Intentions and Capabilities*, ed. Patrick Clawson (Washington, DC: National Defense University, 1994), pp. 27-48.

[20] *JI*, November 2. For the official response from the Foreign Ministry, see *JI*, November 6, 1994.

[21] Ibid., September 11, in *DR*, September 20, 1994.

IRAN AND THE UNITED STATES: EMOTION VS. REASON

Since its ascent to power, the Islamic regime has viewed the United States as "the Great Satan." Animosity toward Washington became a major symbol of the revolution and was "raised . . . to a near religion."[22] Tehran perceived Washington as the primary source of all evils, orchestrating anti-Iranian schemes both regionally (e.g., hostility toward Islamist movements, security policy in the Gulf, support for the peace process, and policy in Central Asia) and domestically (e.g., economic sanctions, support for the opposition, and "cultural onslaught" [*tahajom-e farhangi*]). The radicals set the tone, and to them America was the archenemy of Iran and Islam.[23]

In their public statements, Rafsanjani and Khamene'i demonstrated noticeable differences in their attitudes toward the United States. The Supreme Leader believed that "in the confrontation between Islam and global arrogance [i.e., the West]," the latter would soon "be brought to its knees."[24] He was more concerned with cultural considerations and more contentious than Rafsanjani. He believed that the slogan "Death to America" emanated from "the depths of the being of each and every" Iranian. He excoriated the United States for being arrogant, greedy, insolent, contemptuous of the Iranian nation, and for ceaselessly hatching conspiracies against Muslims. Hatred, he said, "comes from our side, while mischievous enmity emanates from their side."[25] Suspicious of U.S. intentions, he warned that even when "they appear with a deceitful smile," Americans "have a dagger hidden behind their backs and the other hand is ready to plunder." This is "their true nature,"[26] he said, and thus Iranians "have nothing to talk to them about" and "no need for them."[27]

Rafsanjani's approach was more complex—and at times less belligerent—than that of Khamene'i. In 1983, for example, Rafsanjani addressed "the Americans" and noted that, in principle, Iran was ready for relations with all countries (excluding Israel and South Africa) that were willing to have "proper [*sahih*] relations" with Iran.[28] And though they shared belief that Iran should assume leadership of the Muslim and non-aligned worlds, Rafsanjani implied that Ayatollah Khomeini's anti-Western version of non-alignment had harmed Iran, saying that "the use of an inappropriate method . . . [had] created enemies for our country."[29]

---

[22] Robert Snyder, "Explaining the Iranian Revolution's Hostility Toward the United States," *Journal of South Asian and Middle Eastern Studies* 17, no. 3 (spring 1994), p. 19.

[23] See, for example, *Resalat,* December 28, 1992, in *DR,* January 12, 1993.

[24] *Salam,* August 23, 1992; IRNA, August 23, in *DR,* August 24, 1992.

[25] Radio Tehran, November 2, in *DR,* November 3, 1994.

[26] *Echo of Iran,* no. 62 (March 1993), p. 18.

[27] AFP, November 2, in *DR,* November 2, 1994.

[28] *Kayhan* (Tehran), May 14, 1983.

[29] *Ettela'at,* July 3, 1988.

In 1992, however, Rafsanjani complained that the defeat of "one side [i.e., the Soviet Union] in the Cold War" had encouraged "the other side [the United States] to devise means of . . . ensuring [its] absolute dominance."[30] And though he did not deny Iran's interest in economic ties and considered "popular sensitivity" to the issue inappropriate,[31] he stressed that the United States needed to prove its goodwill first—through its deeds.[32] "Everything depends on America correcting her policies," he said.[33] Washington, he later reiterated, should "prove its good intentions so that the road [to better relations] can be paved."[34]

From time to time, Rafsanjani used his allies within the government to send up "trial balloons" to check public opinion. In a 1990 article in *Ettela'at*, Vice President Mohajerani advocated negotiations with the United States. Not to do so, he wrote, was against the interests of the revolution.[35] Three years later, Majlis deputy Sa'id Raja'i Khorasani wrote a letter to Khamene'i similarly advocating relations with Washington. Although the Supreme Leader rejected his opinion, Khorasani said, it was his Islamic duty to express views that he believed were in the best interests of Iran and Islam.[36] In 1994, aware that the idea was still "strongly rejected" and that Khamene'i had repudiated it altogether, Mohajerani reiterated that a direct dialogue was necessary.[37]

Opposition to such proposals was almost universal. Ardebili said that compromise (*mosalehe*) or reconciliation (*sazesh*) with the United States was anti-revolutionary[38] and contradicted the interests of "religion, revolution, and the state."[39] *Salam* saw in Raja'i's letter a reflection of America's "miraculous ability" to influence Iranians' minds.[40] Mohtashami blamed

---

[30] Radio Tehran, September 18, in *DR*, September 20, 1992. Others viewed this new reality as the turning point for a different kind of "new world order." Deputy Foreign Minister 'Abbas Maleki, for example, suggested that Russia should now "view itself as being part of Asia, or at least as a Euro-Asian country" in order to establish "a solid and strong economic and political front against the West," adding that Iran has "the oil, Japan the technology, China the labor, and Central Asian countries the agriculture. Therefore, an intermingling of these economies could bring prosperity to the continent." See *TT*, February 22, 1993.

[31] Tehran TV, February 1, in *DR*, February 3, 1993; AFP, December 19, in *DR*, December 20, 1993.

[32] *Resalat* and *Ettela'at*, June 8, 1994. Similarly, Mohammad Javad Larijani, vice chairman of the Majlis foreign relations committee, contended that it was "the responsibility of our Western partners" to generate a change; see *FT*, February 8, 1993. For similar assertions, see *KI*, February 2, in *DR*, February 2, 1993.

[33] Tehran TV, February 1, in *DR*, February 3, 1993.

[34] Rafsanjani interview, *Middle East Insight* 11, no. 5 (July-August 1995), pp. 7-14.

[35] *Ettela'at*, April 26, 1990.

[36] *Salam*, September 15, in *DR*, October 1, 1993; *IT*, November 5, 1993; *KI*, November 2, 1993; *al-Safir*, November 29, in *DR*, December 14, 1993.

[37] *Al-Majallah*, November 6, 1994.

[38] *Ettela'at*, November 20, 1993.

[39] Ibid., October 9, 1993; *IT*, October 15, 1993.

[40] *Salam*, October 28, 30, 1993.

Rafsanjani for supporting such "deviationist ideas."[41] Faced with such harsh criticism, whatever hopes Rafsanjani had entertained for a *rapprochement* with Washington were "destroyed," his "Westward-looking" policy had "completely failed,"[42] and he was forced to retreat.[43] But even then, he did it in a characteristically obscure way: he asked his associates to deny that Mohajerani's proposals reflected his views.[44]

Though the sobering realities of the damage caused by the two countries' mutual hostility eventually led some Iranian officials to reconsider this entrenched attitude and to try to change the policy, the radicals managed to frustrate them. Just before President Clinton entered office, the *Tehran Times* offered him an olive branch. "Any sign of goodwill will be responded to by goodwill from the Iranian side," it said, adding that it hoped the American president would "take advantage of this golden opportunity."[45] The paper went on to say that ideological differences do not mean "that we intend to be at continual strife" with the United States, and pointed to the recent Iranian-Soviet reconciliation as a "possible solution" for American-Iranian tension as well. Reminding Washington that "Iran used its spiritual influence" to win the release of Western hostages in Lebanon, the *Tehran Times* added that Iran was still waiting for an appropriate U.S. response—and suggested that lifting the freeze on Iranian assets in the United States "would be a proper gesture."[46]

Kayhan responded to these overtures by censuring those who "naively believe" that ties with the United States would "solve all of our problems" and who attempt to disguise the enemy's true nature.[47] *Resalat* similarly dismissed the "theory" that Iran must assimilate into the world system as a *sine qua non* for advancing its economy.[48] Mohtashami criticized those entertaining such ideas as deluded, "bankrupt, Westernized, selfish elements" who are "bereft of intelligence and understanding." Rather than seeking to forge ties as the means to rehabilitate the economy, he maintained, Iran should "vaccinate" itself against Western economic viruses.[49] In a 1995 Friday sermon, Ahmad Jannati made the radical approach clear. "Showing mercy to the 'wolf,'" he said, is only a sign of

---

[41] *Jahan-e Islam*, October 19, in *DR*, November 10, 1993.

[42] *Echo of Iran*, no. 62 (March 1993), pp. 8, 11.

[43] Ibid., no. 61 (February 1993), p. 12.

[44] *JI*, May 1, 1990, wrote that three of his close associates disclosed that they were asked by Rafsanjani to express his displeasure at the publication of the article. For Mohtashami's harsh criticism of Mohajerani's ideas, see *Kayhan* (Tehran), April 29, 1990.

[45] *TT*, January 20, 1993; *NYT*, January 21, 1993.

[46] *TT*, January 13, in *DR*, January 21, 1993.

[47] *Kayhan* (Tehran), February 1, in *DR*, February 12, 1993. See, similarly, ibid., January 28, in *DR*, February 10, 1993.

[48] *Resalat*, November 4, in *DR*, November 20, 1992.

[49] *Salam*, July 27, 1994.

weakness and is unlikely to satisfy the wolf or to rescue the sheep.[50] To the radicals (and often the pragmatists, too), the U.S. "wolf" remained the "mother of all corruption."[51] The harsh criticism of those advocating some kind of *rapprochement* with the United States attests to their existence, but with the radicals setting the tone and having made animosity toward Washington a major element of its policy, the regime found it extremely difficult to change it. The issue was imbued more with sentiment and ideology than logic and national interest.

To a degree, emotions and misconceptions also influenced the American approach to Iran. The 1979 hostage crisis, the Iran-Contra affair, the experience of Americans held hostage by pro-Iranian groups in Lebanon, and Iran's human rights record combined to influence the American public's feelings toward Iran. More recent reasons for official displeasure include Iran's opposition to the Middle East peace process, support for militant Islamists, challenge to moderate regimes in the region, and reported efforts to acquire nuclear weapons. These attitudes have been further encouraged by domestic politics (e.g., initiatives by Congress) and pressure from regional allies such as Israel and moderate Arab countries.

The wide political and cultural differences between the two countries made it difficult for Washington to understand Iran's revolutionary rhetoric and blurred, inconsistent policies. The United States also seemed to be sending mixed signals to Iran, from the fall of the shah to the Iran-Contra affair, and from its "dual containment" policy to the concurrent expansion of economic ties. As a policy, dual containment has certain merits, but its implementation—including half-hearted efforts by the United States itself—lacks the support of U.S. allies and is a leaking sieve.

American rhetoric against Iran is no milder than Iranian discourse. Iran is referred to as an "outlaw nation" and "the world's leading sponsor of terrorism." Thus, Secretary of State Warren Christopher stated, "They have projected terror throughout the region. . . . Wherever you look, you find the evil hand of Iran in this region."[52] Yet despite strong public statements and the dual containment policy, until 1994 economic ties between the two countries actually expanded. The United States (including foreign subsidiaries of U.S. companies) became one of Iran's leading trade partners, accounting for a larger portion of Tehran's total trade than at the peak of the shah's regime. In 1994, American oil companies purchased an estimated $4.25 billion of Iranian oil—33 percent of its total oil exports.[53] The *Economist* referred to U.S.-Iranian relations as

---

[50] Radio Tehran, January 27, in *DR,* January 30, 1995.

[51] IRNA, February 11, in *DR,* February 11, 1993.

[52] Neal M. Sher, *Comprehensive U.S. Sanctions Against Iran: A Plan for Action* (Washington, DC: AIPAC, 1995), p. 16.

[53] Ibid., pp. 27-28.

"a convenient marriage,"[54] and *New York Times* columnist Thomas Friedman called it "feel-good containment—a policy that makes us feel good but doesn't make Iran feel bad enough to change its behavior."[55]

These mixed signals confused both Iran and U.S. allies, and lent further credence to one of Khomeini's chief slogans—"America can't do a damned thing." Moreover, they amounted to an American admission of its failure to contain Iran; one could chant "Death to America" and still do business with it. This not only made it more difficult for Washington to demand that its allies act to contain Iran, but gave them license to expand contacts. Iran did not even attempt to refute reports of its trade with the United States because, as Rafsanjani cynically remarked, "[i]t was beneficial to [Iran's] global policy to make Western countries wonder why the United States, which keeps telling them not to have relations [with Iran], has so many dealings" with Tehran itself.[56]

It was in this context that President Clinton signed an executive order prohibiting all trade with Iran in May 1995. Publicly, Tehran played down the order's effects. Foreign Minister Velayati declared that it had "failed at birth"[57] and Rafsanjani said it "bore no fruit but defeat and shame" for the United States,[58] and only "further strengthened the Iranian economy."[59] *Jomhuri-ye Islami* believed the U.S. trade sanctions would ultimately benefit Iran by demonstrating Washington's failure to organize an anti-Iranian front and dealing the final blow to Iranians who had entertained ideas of improving relations.[60] Although Tehran did not voice its anxiety, the sanctions did raise concerns. Had Washington's allies joined in its efforts to contain Iran, Rafsanjani conceded, they would have had "some effect" on Iran's economy.[61] As it was, the sanctions did inflict a psychological blow on the economy and trigger a crisis of confidence in Iran. This was perhaps best exemplified by the sharp decline in the value of the riyal, which shrank from around 2,500 to the dollar in January 1995 to about 4,300 in April and around 6,500 by May 10. Concerned by the possible ramifications of this trend, the government banned the free market in foreign exchange, announced a new official rate (3,000 riyals to the dollar) and took administrative measures to impose it. The riyal then stabilized at around 5,000 to the dollar. In the absence of a concerted sanctions effort, Iran could get what it needed from other countries, but Rafsanjani still seemed to regret that Clinton had passed up opportunities to improve ties.

---

[54] *Economist*, February 25, 1995.

[55] *NYT*, March 29, 1995.

[56] Tehran TV, May 9, in *DR*, May 16, 1995.

[57] Radio Monte Carlo, May 5, in *DR*, May 8, 1995.

[58] Radio Tehran, July 26, in *DR*, July 27, 1995.

[59] IRNA, July 27, in *DR*, July 27, 1995.

[60] *JI*, May 3, 1995.

[61] Tehran TV, May 9, in *DR*, May 16, 1995. See also Gary Sick, "A Sensitive Policy Toward Iran," *Middle East Insight* 11, no. 5 (July-August 1995), pp. 21-22.

Iran's business deals with American firms, he maintained, were "a message" that Washington had not correctly understood.[62]

Critics of American policy have argued that given Iran's geopolitical importance and evolving internal political and economic situation, the United States would be wise to "keep the door open" to contacts.[63] "Iran is Ripe for a Peaceful Overture" was the title of one article, the author of which dismissed as "a pipedream" the "notion that we are going to drive Iran into bankruptcy and thereby bring down the Islamic government."[64] Washington's "obstruction of international development credits for Iran will neither transform nor bring down" the Islamic regime, he wrote;[65] America's allies will simply complete the trade deals that it abandons. "Economically, Iran is not going to be hurt" by the sanctions, argued another commentator. "And politically, they will strengthen the regime" by becoming "a rallying cry for the government." This, in turn, could discredit the pragmatists and bring "more hardline attitudes and leaders to the fore."[66]

Some have argued that growing hardships within Iran could even lead the *current* regime to greater extremism, in order to satisfy factional rivals and divert public opinion from domestic failures. Indeed, Europe and Japan have justified their alternative approach to Iran on the grounds that the clerical regime "is not made up only of radicals" and it is "necessary to support the moderates."[67] According to proponents of this view, "if Iran is not economically successful, it will become more radical."[68] In fact, "critical dialogue" (as the European alternative to dual containment is known) may have had some influence—its supporters justly take credit for being instrumental in organizing visits to Iran by human rights observers and facilitating an exchange of Hezbollah prisoners for the bodies of Israeli soldiers. Moreover, it is impossible to know what might have happened had there been no dialogue at all.

Overall, however, critical dialogue has failed to produce any significant breakthrough or change in Iranian policy (e.g., its attitude toward the West, the Middle East peace process, the *fatwa* against Salman Rushdie, or support for militant Islamists). French Prime Minister Edouard Balladur made clear that France's desire "to respect human rights" is mitigated by the fact that it has "an economic position to defend" and seeks "a good

---

[62] *IHT*, May 17, 1995.

[63] Edward P. Djerejian, "The Prospects for U.S.-Iranian Relations," *Middle East Insight* 11, no. 5 (July-August 1995), pp. 4-5.

[64] Sick, "A Sensitive Policy Toward Iran," pp. 21-22; and "Iran is Ripe for a Peaceful Overture," *LAT*, November 17, 1994.

[65] Sick, *LAT*, November 17, 1994.

[66] *LAT*, May 2, 1995.

[67] Remarks by Japanese Prime Minister Tomiichi Murayama, *MEED*, January 27, 1995; *LAT*, February 15, 1995. See also Patrick Clawson, *Business as Usual? Western Policy Options Toward Iran* (Washington, DC: American Jewish Congress, 1995), p. 35.

[68] Kazuo Takahashi, quoted in Clawson, *Business as Usual?*, p. 34.

balance" between the two. Thus, "whatever Iran may say, and perhaps do, the commercial self-interest of competing nations" will ultimately work in its favor.[69] Iran seems to have drawn confidence from the lack of concerted Western policy and seen no pressing need to moderate its policy.

Though the difficulties of imposing effective sanctions unilaterally are self-evident, the likelihood that an accommodative approach (which is often perceived as weakness) will influence Tehran is equally questionable. All governments (and particularly revolutionary ones) are reluctant to cede their professed doctrines voluntarily; an economically stronger Iran is hardly more likely to retreat from its guiding dogma than a weakened one. Moreover, having already deviated from so many ideological convictions (e.g., accepting the ceasefire with Iraq, foreign loans, Syria's participation in the peace process, and family planning), it would be politically difficult for the clerical regime to retreat from the few remaining elements of its core doctrine, such as spurning ties with the United States and maintaining its animosity toward Israel. Thus, the Islamic Republic's challenge to the region is likely to persist as long as it retains its current ideological tenets.

A senior U.S. official explained American policy as an attempt to encourage Tehran "to make a strategic choice." Washington is "still willing to engage in a dialogue with authoritative representatives" of Iran, she said. "We believe that pressure and dialogue can go together."[70] They probably can. What is missing on both sides are more concrete conditions for changing policy toward the other side. For its part, the United States should have offered more "carrots" to go with the "stick" in its statements directed toward the Islamic Republic. As far as Iran is concerned, the problem is not merely whether Rafsanjani genuinely wants such a change, but the degree to which he is capable of leading Iran in that direction. Rafsanjani seems to have been more effective in shaping Iran's policy while serving under Khomeini than as president himself. Those who supported Rafsanjani in the 1996 Majlis elections may have been aware of the need to improve relations with the United States, but it is unclear whether they are capable of implementing such a policy. At this stage, they seem afraid to even publicly suggest such an idea.

PRAGMATISM IN THE 'NEAR ABROAD'

Iran's foreign policy has generally been more pragmatic toward its neighbors and more militant farther away. This approach to Iran's "near abroad" was best illustrated by its lack of support for the 1991 Shi'i uprising in Iraq. Despite their sectarian affinity, the rebels' pledge to form

---

[69] *FT*, April 30, 1994; Clawson, *Business as Usual?*, p. 30.

[70] Ellen Laipson, *et al.*, "U.S. Policy Toward Iran: From Containment to Relentless Pursuit," *Middle East Policy* 4, nos. 1-2 (1995), p. 2.

an Islamic republic, common hatred of Saddam Hussein and the Ba'th regime, and shared obligation to the *mostaz'afin*, Tehran did not come unequivocally or even substantially to the aid of the Iraqi Shi'a. The clerical regime had sound reasons for its reluctance: it doubted they would succeed, and knew that supporting a losing cause would harm its larger interests. Once again, Iran placed its national interests ahead of the ideology of the revolution.[71]

Tehran pursued a similar policy toward the Muslim former Soviet republics on its northern border. Though it sought to maintain good relations with these governments, it was careful not to antagonize Moscow and to maintain regional stability. The fact that none of the republics' leaders was an ideal Islamic ruler and that they generally maintained close ties with Turkey, the United States, and Israel did not preclude close ties with Tehran. Though Iran strove to expand its ideological influence (particularly in Tajikistan), this was not its highest priority. The dichotomy between pragmatism close to home and radicalism farther afield is perhaps best exemplified by Iran's contrasting approaches to the crises in Nagorno-Karabakh and Bosnia. In the former, Tehran sought to mediate with a view to preventing instability; in the latter, it took a more militant line.[72] Though its ideology and ambitions obliged Tehran to demonstrate its "revolutionary presence" throughout the world, its policy succeeded in combining radical doctrine with a healthy dose of national interest.

The general pattern has thus been the use of pragmatic policy to perpetuate a radical regime. Occasionally, pragmatic considerations have even led to a *more* radical approach in selective fields; after all, pragmatism is not necessarily synonymous with moderation. The ideology of the revolution tends to encourage greater radicalism, but is usually balanced by the more pragmatic interests of the state. When the interests of the state (as perceived by the ruling elite) champion radicalism, however, there is no domestic counterbalance. Moreover, pragmatists and radicals share a general vision of Iran as an Islamic state and a leading regional power. Thus, like its domestic policy, Iran's regional policy also continues to be two-tiered, complex, and dynamic.

---

[71] Iran also did not support a rebellion by Iraqi Kurds, presumably for the opposite reason: fear that they might succeed, which would have been contrary to Iran's national interests.

[72] But even in this regard, some Iranians warned that military support for the Bosnian Muslims might backfire and harm broader Islamic interests. The *Tehran Times*, for example, described Velayati's plea for support for the Muslims at the November 1992 meeting of the Islamic Conference Organization in Jeddah, Saudi Arabia, as "miscalculated and unwise," since it would only "push the Catholic Croats and Orthodox Serbs to unite against Muslim Bosnians" and lead to their "total annihilation"; see *TT*, December 2, in *DR*, December 9, 1992.

An Iranian citizen similarly challenged Rafsanjani's November 1995 call for support for the Muslims of Bosnia on economic grounds—i.e., that it would be appropriate if Iranians themselves enjoyed a minimum degree of welfare, but given that they could not meet the essential needs of Iran's children, they could not even consider offering such help abroad; see *Salam*, December 9, 1995.

IRAN, ISLAMISM, AND THE PEACE PROCESS

One area in which Tehran's policy has been consistently radical is its support for Islamist movements which, to varying degrees, have drawn inspiration and encouragement from the Iranian revolution. Tehran sees itself as the "mother of all Islamic revolutions" and feels a commitment to encourage, guide, and support them. Although Iran's attitude toward and actual support for various Islamist movements differs (and has changed over the course of the revolution and among different domestic groups), its commitment to these groups has remained generally consistent.[73] Tehran regards their success as a tribute to its own revolution, a manifestation of its influence, and a symbol of its Islamic dominance.

Khomeini viewed his ascendance as a stage in (and an instrument of) an overall Islamic revolution. "Our movement strives for an *Islamic* goal, not for Iran alone. . . . Iran is [only] the starting point."[74] Although this doctrine has undergone some changes, it remains valid for many in Iran. In 1992, for example, SNDC member Mohammad Javad Larijani promised that "the cresting of Islamic movement will soon transform the face of the world" in the same manner as the Renaissance changed Europe.[75] Just as the Renaissance "brought new fundamentals" of legitimacy, freedom, and scientific progress to the West, so Islamism—launched from Iran—will have a similar impact, he said. "We shall be the watchmen of this immense ideological political movement. We will pave the way for the expansion and deepening of contemporary Islamism."[76] Thus, many Iranian officials felt that Islamist movements deserved moral encouragement and material support. For their part, these movements view Iran as a source of inspiration and support. Despite its faults and limitations, Iran remains a successful model of people, led by clerics and inspired by Islam, toppling a regime with a powerful army and the support of a superpower.

But the lesson of the Iranian revolution was not restricted to Islamists. It made a strong impression on local regimes and foreign powers as well. The 1979 revolution caught the shah by surprise; he failed to comprehend or respond to the Islamist challenge. Similarly, foreign powers neither encouraged the shah to act nor would have allowed him the freedom to do so. (This does not necessarily imply that it would have been possible to reverse the process.) Since the revolution, local governments have become more aware of the Islamist threat and determined to confront it—and the outside world more tolerant of oppressive measures to do so. (Algeria is one such example.) Thus, while the Iranian revolution encouraged other Islamist movements, it also created significant barriers to their ultimate success. Governments are aware of the challenge, have developed the

---

[73] See Menashri, "Khomeini's Vision: Nationalism or World Order?" pp. 40-57.

[74] See interviews in *al-Mustaqbal*, January 13, 1979; Radio Tehran, May 7, in *DR*, May 8, 1979.

[75] *Resalat*, December 14, in *DR*, December 21, 1992.

[76] *Ettela'at*, December 31, 1992, in *DR*, January 22, 1993.

necessary countermeasures, and are fighting back. Though this does not ensure their success, it is an indication of their awareness and effort.

Although Iran has no border with Israel, no territorial claims on it, and no role in any of the Arab-Israeli wars, since the revolution it has become an active player in the conflict. Viewing itself as the leading Islamic power and seeking centrality in the Middle East, it felt a duty to provide leadership to the opponents of the peace process. Whereas the Arab states consider the conflict a political-national dispute, Iran sees it as a religious crusade. Tehran rejects Israel's right to exist. It views the conflict as involving two diametrically opposed powers: absolute good embodied in Islam, and blasphemy as personified by its rivals, with no compromise possible—in Iran's view, one side must be annihilated in order for the other to survive. It is therefore Iran's duty to lead and support the believers' camp. This is not only consistent with the ideology of the revolution but also compatible with the interests of the state as perceived by the ruling elite.

Strategically, the Arab-Israeli dispute provided Tehran with a context to demonstrate regional leadership. With the other rejectionist states having receded from the scene—as a result of strategic choice (Syria), military defeat (Iraq), or marginality (Libya)—Iran sees its continued leadership of the anti-Israel campaign as a means of enhancing its credentials as a major regional power, coinciding with its ambitions. Moreover, Tehran's rejectionist stance offers certain domestic advantages. Focusing on its leading role in remote issues helps divert public attention from domestic problems and demonstrates regional centrality and ideological adherence (thereby satisfying the radicals)—all for a relatively low political price. By contrast, abandoning its consistent support for the Islamists' struggle would harm Iran's regional plans and alienate certain segments at home.

The Israeli-PLO Declaration of Principles provided Iran with an even better opportunity to assert its claim of Islamic leadership. Tehran viewed the peace process as treachery (*khiyanat*) against Islam[77] and a contradiction of Islamic aims,[78] and claimed that Arab leaders had abandoned their duty to confront Israel and that it alone continued to hoist the flag of Palestine. Iran organized and led the anti-peace camp, calling for a *jihad* to save Palestine and convening an International Conference to Support the Islamic Revolution to coincide with the October 1991 Madrid peace conference. When the Oslo accords were signed, Tehran pledged to spare no expense to defeat them, promised "limitless support" for other opponents of the agreements,[79] and convened

[77] See Yazdi's statement in *Ettela'at*, September 11, 1993; *IT*, September 17, 1993.

[78] *Ettela'at*, September 14, 1993. See, similarly, *Kayhan* (Tehran), September 15, in *DR*, October 13, 1993; *Ettela'at*, September 18 and 19, 1993; *Jahan-e Islam*, September 18, in *DR*, September 30, 1993.

[79] *Ettela'at*, September 11, 1993; *IT*, September 17, 1993.

another conference on Palestine in October 1993. Tehran continued to support the Lebanese Hezbollah in its struggle against Israel and backed Hamas (including reports of financial support and training of activists) and the Islamic Jihad.[80] Not only that it did not condemn acts of terrorism against Israel, it regarded them as acts of martyrdom (*shehadat-talabane*) which, it claimed, is the only language Jews understand and the only path to secure the legitimate rights of the Palestinians.[81]

At the same time, however, SNDC Secretary Hasan Ruhani noted that Tehran was "not seeking to pursue any military action" of its own against "this shameful accord."[82] Given its own domestic difficulties, limited ability to reverse the trend, and the fact that the Palestinians were making the move of their own choice, many Iranians doubted the advisability of being more pro-Palestine than the Palestinians (or other Arabs).

---

[80] See *MECS* 1991, pp. 194-98; *MECS* 1993, pp. 136-38, 408-10.

[81] *Resalat*, January, 23, 1994; *Kayhan* (Tehran), January 24, 1994; *Ettela'at*, February 26 and March 1, 1994; Radio Tehran, February 26, in *DR*, February 28, 1994.

[82] IRNA, September 22, in *DR*, September 23, 1993; *Ettela'at*, October 7, in *DR*, October 18, 1993. *Salam* lamented that when officials move away from public forums, they distance themselves from the firm stances expected of them; see *Salam*, September 26 and, similarly, October 3, in *DR*, October 7, 1993; *JI*, September 27, in *DR*, October 6, 1993.

VIII

The Islamic Revolution: End of the Dream?

Despite considerable pragmatic deviations from the doctrine of the revolution, the Islamic Republic has thus far demonstrated no significant success in solving Iran's social, economic, and political problems. Ideologically, the regime has abandoned its path. It may still be called the "rule of the *ayatollahs*," but Iran is no longer actually governed by genuine theologians, nor is its course shaped by purely ideological considerations. "People feel they've been betrayed," said Ibrahim Yazdi, and "that the revolution has been kidnapped."[1] In a way, it was in fact hijacked by religio-politicians who (by Khomeini's own standards) lack the legitimacy to rule.

Various observers have pointed to the regime's multi-faceted failures, claiming that the very basis of the Islamic revolution, not merely the politics of the regime, is being challenged. Hashim concludes that Iran faces "an existential crisis" that includes "a variety of acute pressures and threats to its political legitimacy, domestic stability and national security." It is "ideologically bankrupt, economically and morally exhausted, militarily weak, increasingly unpopular domestically, . . . and friendless abroad."[2] Banuazizi adds that it is "becoming more and more ideologically rigid, economically unstable, politically repressive, and internationally isolated."[3] Lamote claims that domestic difficulties—withering grassroots support and eroding legitimacy—threaten to "bring down" the regime.[4] Similarly, Shirley comments that the revolution "has failed, dismaying its people and bankrupting its coffers." For the poor, "the revolution and its utopian hopes are dead."[5] Even 'Abdi maintains that the revolution has "failed to change the political structure of the country" and the gulf between the people and the government is as wide as during the days of the shah[6]—no minor criticism from such a devout revolutionary.

---

[1] *IHT*, May 31, 1995.

[2] Ahmed Hashim, *The Crisis of the Iranian State*, Adelphi Paper 296 (London: International Institute for Strategic Studies, 1995), p. 3.

[3] Ali Banuazizi, "Iran's Revolutionary Impasse: Political Factionalism and Societal Resistance," *Middle East Report* 24, no. 191 (November-December 1994), p. 2.

[4] Laurent Lamote [pseudonym], "Domestic Politics and Strategic Intentions," in *Iran's Strategic Intentions and Capabilities*, ed. Patrick Clawson (Washington, DC: National Defense University, 1994), pp. 6-8, 24.

[5] Edward G. Shirley [pseudonym], "Fundamentalism in Power: Is Iran's Present Algeria's Future?" *Foreign Affairs* 74, no. 3 (May-June 1995), pp. 35, 39. See also Shirley, "The Iran Policy Trap," *Foreign Policy*, no. 96 (fall 1994), p. 93.

[6] *CSM*, April 20, 1995.

Clearly, support for the Islamic regime is diminishing. There is a sense of exhaustion, saturation with revolutionary excess, and a concomitant "loss of zeal."[7] If declining attendance in mosques and pro-government rallies is a barometer of popular alienation, the government faces a serious problem.[8] Islamic *khoms* and *zakat* (alms) from the faithful have decreased and the clergy's image has been "deeply tarnished."[9] Moreover, politics and Islam "are now clearly separated in the minds of many who not long ago would have used religious vocabulary to describe their aspirations."[10] Manifestations of disenchantment have become more evident, as expressed in the presidential elections, riots in several cities, and growing public criticism.

A retreat from the Islamic norms and principles sanctioned by the revolution is similarly evident. *New York Times* correspondent Elaine Sciolino described Iran as "a country of broken promises" and noted that "the religious oratory that once drove a nation into the streets" now fails to inspire.[11] *Los Angeles Times* reporter Robin Wright observes that the regime's attempt to prohibit private satellite dishes was a great challenge because it pit the "*mullah*cracy" against popular American television programs such as *Oprah* and *L.A. Law*[12]—which, according to Lamis Andoni have become "a symbol of defiance" for Iranians who are fed up with the imposition of strict Islamic law.[13] Even the Iranian monthly *Me'yar* had to concede that many high school students deride the values of Islam and the revolution while expressing admiration for the symbols (e.g., movies, music, T-shirts) of Western culture.[14]

There have already been considerable deviations from some of the most basic elements in Khomeini's philosophy and clear signs of failures in the actual running of the state. These troubles do not necessarily portend the imminent demise of clerical rule, however. Paradoxically, the greater the deviations from dogma (and concomitant adaptability to new realities), the greater the likelihood that the Islamic regime will continue. The revolution may have lost its spirit, but not its muscle and determination to struggle for its survival. Unlike the shah, the Islamic regime is aware of the threats it faces and is fighting for its existence, to the point of ruthlessly suppressing its contenders. Considering the challenges facing the clerics since at least 1981, they have demonstrated an impressive measure of

---

[7]   Shahram Chubin, *Iran's National Security Policy: Capabilities, Intentions, and Impact* (Washington, DC: Carnegie Endowment, 1994), p. 67.

[8]   Hashim, p. 25; Shirley, "The Iran Policy Trap," p. 83; Olivier Roy, *The Failure of Political Islam* (Cambridge, MA: Harvard University Press, 1994), p. 199.

[9]   Lamote, p. 12.

[10]   Shirley, "The Iran Policy Trap," p. 87.

[11]   *IHT*, May 31, 1995.

[12]   *LAT*, March 14, 1995.

[13]   *CSM*, April 28, 1995.

[14]   *Me'yar*, July-August 1995.

political resilience and continuity. To maintain their position, however, they will have to address the myriad of problems, mainly in the economy, relatively soon.

Professor of Islamic philosophy Hojjat ul-Islam Mohsen Kadivar says that the vast majority of clerics in Iran suffer from the growing unpopularity of the clergy, which is held collectively responsible for the mistakes and violations of the few who wield power.[15] Islam is now seen as the "official ideology; and the clergy, no longer as the savior of the people but as the state's agents." The gap between the clergy and the population, "between the imposed Islamic culture and the evolving Iranian society," has widened and exemplifies the "obvious failure of political Islam."[16] The "*mullahs* are now in retreat as public opinion turns hostile. The Iranian revolution is turning on its priests."[17]

Public debates in the Majlis and in the press are now "questioning the very notion of clerical rule." The practices of the revolution, "in the view of many, are giving Islam a bad name."[18] A "growing array of political interest groups, intellectuals and even some *mullahs* argue that it's time for the clergy to begin sharing power or step aside." A "large number of clerics are now against the clergy in power," a former government official said. "They now think it was a mistake to take government office."[19] Although many may share such feelings, few dare to publicly express them. Former Minister of Islamic Guidance Mohammad Khatami feared that the realities established under the Islamic regime "endanger Islam."[20] Shortly before he passed away, Bazargan warned that "the main threat to Islam in Iran today is the experience of the people under the Islamic government."[21]

The impact of such failures, many Iranians fear, may extend far from Iran's borders and discourage Islamists elsewhere. The essence of such a challenge was encapsulated in a penetrating question put to Rafsanjani by a journalist. Although Iranian policy is based on Islam, he said, the situation in Iran is no better than in other developing countries. How is it then possible, he asked, to regard Islam as the best guide to solving the country's problems?[22] This does not necessarily mean that Islamism has lost its appeal. Given the harsh realities that people experience in different parts of the Muslim world, the Iranian example can still attract the minds and souls of young Islamists. Regardless of the apparent failure of Islamist

---

[15] Eric Rouleau, "The Islamic Republic of Iran: Paradoxes and Contradictions in a Changing Society," *Middle East Insight* 11, no. 5 (July-August 1995), p. 56.

[16] Lamote, pp. 7-9.

[17] *LAT*, December 13, 1994.

[18] Gary Sick, "A Sensitive Policy Toward Iran," *Middle East Insight* 11, no. 5 (July-August 1995), pp. 21-22.

[19] *LAT*, June 6, 1995. See also Soroush's views in Chapter 2.

[20] Lamote, p. 12.

[21] Interview with Bazargan in *Kiyan* 11 (March-May 1993).

[22] *Ettela'at*, June 8, 1994.

rule—in Iran as in Sudan—to solve problems facing the people, they may prefer to look at the full half of the glass: the Iranian revolution's success in toppling the shah. In fact, the Iranian example has proven that its ideology can be an efficient means of inciting people *against* policies and rulers, but a less potent tool *for* constructive solutions and effective governance.

Seventeen years after the Iranian revolution, its ideology is waning, its political system has thus far failed to remedy Iran's social and economic malaise, and the number of disillusioned Iranians grows daily. The stability of the regime seems to depend less on the degree of return to Islam than on the government's ability to satisfy the expectations that initially brought it to power. This is the revolution's main challenge, and it is in this area that significant progress has yet to be achieved.

THE WASHINGTON INSTITUTE POLICY PAPERS SERIES

THE WASHINGTON INSTITUTE POLICY FOCUS SERIES

RECENT PUBLICATIONS OF THE WASHINGTON INSTITUTE

The Future of U.S.-Israel Strategic Cooperation—An examination by Shai Feldman of the origins of U.S.-Israel strategic cooperation and the ways in which America's victory in the Cold War and progress in the Arab-Israeli peace process can be used to build a closer, more integrated bilateral defense relationship in the years ahead.

Making Peace with the PLO: The Rabin Government's Road to the Oslo Accord— A detailed assessment of the personal, domestic, and international factors that led Yitzhak Rabin, Shimon Peres, and Israel's Labor government to conduct the secret negotiations that resulted in the historic Israeli-Palestinian peace accords, by *Jerusalem Post* and *U.S. News and World Report* correspondent David Makovsky.

Democracy and Arab Political Culture—An examination by Elie Kedourie of the political traditions of Islam and the introduction of Western ideas into the Middle East in the 19th century.

Supporting Peace: America's Role in an Israel-Syria Peace Agreement—A report by Michael Eisenstadt, Andrew Bacevich, and Carl Ford on the role that U.S. forces could play in monitoring and maintaining an Israel-Syria peace agreement.

The Politics of Change in the Middle East—A collection of essays examining regional political stability and regime succession, edited by Robert Satloff. Contributors include Ami Ayalon, Amatzia Baram, Shaul Bakhash, Adam Garfinkle, Emile Nakleh, Itamar Rabinovich, and Barry Rubin.

Peacewatch: The Arab-Israeli Peace Process and U.S. Policy—A comprehensive analysis and documentary record of the Arab-Israeli peace process from January 1993 to March 1994, by the scholars and associates of the Washington Institute.

Democracy in the Middle East: Defining the Challenge—A collections of essays exploring the problems and opportunities that a policy of promoting democracy would create for U.S. interests. Contributors include Graham Fuller, Mohammed Abdelbeki Hermassi, Martin Kramer, Joshua Muravchik, and Laurie Mylroie.

UN Security Council Resolution 242: The Building Block of Peacemaking—A collection of essays examining the resolution's history and relevance for current Arab-Israeli negotiations, featuring Adnan Abu Odeh, Nabil Elaraby, Meir Rosenne, Eugene Rostow, Dennis Ross, and Vernon Turner.

For a complete catalogue of Washington Institute publications, contact:

The Washington Institute *for Near East Policy*
1828 L Street, NW, Suite 1050
Washington, D.C. 20036
Phone (202) 452-0650 ◊ Fax (202) 223-5364
E-mail: info@washingtoninstitute.org